With Love

FROM DAD

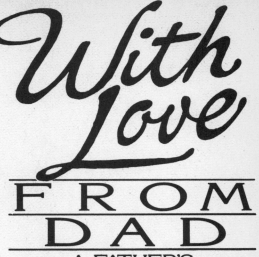

With Love

FROM
DAD

A FATHER'S
REFLECTIONS
ON LIFE

JUDSON
EDWARDS

HARVEST HOUSE PUBLISHERS
Eugene, Oregon 97402

With Love FROM DAD

Copyright © 1986 by Harvest House Publishers
Eugene, Oregon 97402

Library of Congress Catalog Card Number 85-081939
ISBN 0-89081-501-1

Printed in the United States of America.

To
Stacy and Randel

With Love

FROM
DAD

CONTENTS

CONTENTS

A WORD OF APOLOGY

It has suddenly dawned on me that in a couple of years both of you probably will be gone from home. Your mother and I will then have to adjust to life in an "empty nest," and I'm afraid it could be a rough transition. For years we have built our lives around ball practice, homework, shopping trips, dental appointments, haircuts, family meals, and school activities. When you leave we will have to figure out what to do with all our spare time. We may be bored silly!

Our time together as a family has passed far too quickly for me. Wasn't it just yesterday that we walked you across the street to start kindergarten? I distinctly remember your excitement at the prospect of school and our vain attempt to fight back a mysterious mist that kept filling our

eyes. And soon we will escort you to a college dormitory and repeat the whole scene again. Yours has been the shortest childhood in the annals of time!

I had so much good advice and many thrilling experiences I wanted to give you, but now I sadly realize that much will have to go unsaid and undone. So, to make up for those missed opportunities, I've decided to write you a series of letters. Each Saturday morning for the next year I'm going to sit down here at the kitchen table beside a steaming pot of coffee and string together some pearls of wisdom to give you. These ramblings may well represent the wisdom of a fool, but I hope they'll help you, both now and in the future. As we have opportunity, I hope we can talk about some of these things.

The first letter needs to be, I think, a word of apology. In reflecting on our relationship, I feel a need to say "I'm sorry" for a few things.

I need to apologize first for calling you "kids." I know you're both nearly grown, and that in some ways you're more mature than I am. But you'll always be the "kids" to me. Even when you're my age and have teenagers of your own you'll still be the "kids." In trying to decide on a salutation for these epistles, I just felt more comfortable writing "Dear Kids" than anything else. Don't take that as a slight; take it as a promise that you'll never escape my affection.

Second, I need to apologize for having to write these things in a letter. It would be better to talk about these ideas and to verbally express my feelings to you. But I can write ideas and especially feelings easier than I can say them. As you know, our family has not been famous for its verbal expression. We have chosen to show our love in more subtle ways. For example, we have not said "I love you" very much; we have chosen instead to call each other weird nicknames! We've not kissed very often either; we've adopted the policy of slapping hands and "giving five!" In truth, we seldom speak our feelings at all; we show them through little kindnesses we try to do for each other.

In a way, though, I regret that we're not more "showy" with our affection, and wish we were not so private with our feelings. The only justification I can find for our behavior is that our family life has been sacred to us, and sacred things are sometimes cheapened by too many words.

I want to apologize to you also for all the times I have taken out my personal frustrations on you. More times than I care to remember, you have received the anger that should have been directed elsewhere. Parents have a tendency to vent their hostility on their children, and regrettably I have vented on you occasionally. That means you have received several unjustified spankings and numerous misplaced tongue-lashings through the years. Here, on a Saturday morning silent but for the gurgle of the coffeepot, I can reflect on my wrongs and admit them. This doesn't mean, however, that I'll never again speak a cross, irritable word to you. Give me enough pressure, and I'll probably take aim again! When that happens, I hope you'll remember this apology and just say, "Dad must be having a tough time right now." Can I use this letter as an insurance policy to cover all future irritability?

Finally, I feel I should apologize for assuming the posture of "the resident expert on life" in these letters. In all honesty, I'm not much of an expert on anything. Like you, I'm still groping for truth, I still have dark days of discouragement, and I'm still trying to "get my life together." In fact, these letters are probably more for my benefit than for yours. You may not need to read these things, but I need to write them. I need you to know what I'm feeling and what I wish for you when you leave home. So don't see these letters as a foolproof guide to successful living. See them as random love notes from a father with silly mist in his eyes.

Later,

Dad

THE MAN WITH
THE STEAM ENGINE

Thursday night on the ten o'clock news there was a brief human interest story about a man fascinated by steam-engine trains. This man (now in his sixties, I would guess) has had a longtime love affair with steam engines and even bought one of his own some years ago. Occasionally he fires it up and chugs through town, waving at wide-eyed children startled at the sight of an old train engine huffing and puffing down their street. When the man spoke to the interviewer about steam-engine trains, his whole being radiated excitement.

After watching that TV piece, I was amazed that I felt so emotionally uplifted. My spirits rose considerably, and later I wondered why. Why would a TV spot about a

man in love with steam engines cheer me up? The answer to that question, I realize now, is something I want to pass along to you.

Contrary to medical experts, the most dangerous disease in our society is neither cancer nor heart disease, as awful as those diseases are. The most devastating illness around is *indifference*. In the Middle Ages this condition was dubbed "acedia" or sloth, and it was listed by the church as one of the seven deadly sins. The most obvious symptom of acedia is a repeated shrug of the shoulders. When one is afflicted with this condition, nothing matters very much. Cars go unwashed, beds unmade, books unread, children undisciplined, and steam engines unnoticed. Life is a meaningless treadmill.

When acedia gets in its advanced stages, a person is powerless to do much of anything. Like a starving child too weak to brush the flies from his face, the person with severe acedia is too apathetic to see wonder in even life's finest treasures. Sunsets bring no awe, good music stirs no heartstrings, and speckled puppies evoke no chuckles. The medical examiner would never officially declare it, but the person who gets to that point is dead. There is no telling how many dead people are walking the streets today. Acedia is lethal!

The only antidote for the disease is *caring*. You need to start now caring about things — old books, baseball cards, coins, vegetable gardens, or anything else that catches your fancy. If you start now and keep caring, you'll never know the dreadful effects of acedia. You'll always have a corner of the world you can run to and find delight, even though apathy is taking its toll on others.

Here's a quote from a book I like that says it well:

> The tinfoil collectors and the fancy ribbon savers may be absurd, but they're not crazy. They are the ones who still retain the capacity for wonder that is the root of caring. When a little boy finds an old electric motor on a junk

heap, he is pierced to the heart by the weight, the wind-ings, and the silent turning of it. When he gets home, his mother tells him to throw it out. Most likely he will cry. It is his first and truest reaction to the affluent soci-ety. He usually forgets it, but we shouldn't. He is sane; society isn't. He possesses because he *cares*. We don't.[1]

Let's hear it, then, for all those people who, like the little boy with his motor, really care:

The farmer painstakingly plowing his field;
the housewife making cinnamon rolls from scratch;
the nursing home lady hand-stitching her pillowcase.
The infant playing with her toes;
the carpenter crafting his cabinets;
and last, but certainly not least, the gentleman
whistling around town in his steam-engine train.

All of them have one thing in common: They're refusing to fall prey to acedia!

Yours for a life
of fascination,

CONFESSIONS OF A BOOKAHOLIC

It's time to confess: I have a serious addiction. You have known it all along, but I need to admit it and get it out in the open: I'm a bookaholic, a hopelessly hooked bibliomaniac.

The symptoms of this addiction are many, and I have all of them:

· A continual desire to visit bookstores. Employees at the local bookstores know me by my first name. Whenever I get discouraged, I head for one of these stores to do some casual

browsing, and it always does wonders for me. Just being in the vicinity of books is tonic for the true bookaholic.

• A mysterious need to "experience" books. Let me explain. Normal people read books. Bookaholics feel the texture of the pages, sniff the glue in the binding, count the words on a page, and memorize the names of the author and publisher. Just examining, caressing, and smelling a book gives the dyed-in-the-wool bibliomaniac a thrill.

• A deep yearning to write a book. Most bookaholics would swap their firstborn child for the joy of giving birth to a book. For them, the ecstasy of finding a long-sought-after book on a dusty shelf in a used bookstore is surpassed only by the ecstasy of getting an acceptance letter from a publishing company. I know this publishing yearning well, and I have spent hours and hours flailing away at the old typewriter in my study. So far, publishers have been blind to my genius, and the acceptance letters have been rare. But I will keep trying because I am obsessed with the writing and making of books. By the way, no publisher would accept either of you in exchange for printing my work.

• An uncontrollable inclination to buy books. Advanced bookaholics will spend their lunch money on a desired book. They will also wear outdated clothes, drive an antiquated car, or never move to the ritzy suburbs if that's what it takes to enhance their personal library. True bibliomaniacs know that the only safe way to enter a bookstore is with empty pockets.

You have detected all of these symptoms in me, and now I have admitted my disease to you. My particular weakness is theology books, and I have lined the shelves with them. But I also have a smattering of novels, Westerns, psychology treatises, and cookbooks in my collection. In short, I am a sucker for just about anything between two covers! But just so you'll better understand my behavior and just in case either of you has inherited this affliction (and both of you have some of the early signs), let me offer you this brief rationalization. Bookaholics such as myself can make a strong case (at least in our minds!) for our love affair with the printed page.

Why Books Are a Wonderment!

Every book is a visible expression of somebody's "insides," a portrait of a personality.

Every book has a style and perspective all its own. No two books say the same thing or express truth in the same way.

Every book offers the opportunity for learning.

Through books we have access to the finest minds and spirits in history.

Every book grants freedom. Books give us total liberty to move at our own pace, to agree or disagree, to continue reading or to toss them in the trash. Unlike speeches, conversations, and other forms of communication, books give us "distance" and respect our privacy.

Every book is an invitation to silence, a beckoning to flee the noise of the world.

Every book can be saved and treasured, referred back to, marked up, read to a friend, or passed along to someone. Books *last*.

Every book is a concert of skillful people — writer, editor, artist, printer, binder, marketer, reader — all singing the same tune.

Every book has the potential to escort us into a better world, to cause sagging spirits to soar, to make grieving souls smile, to teach wayward minds the truth, to stir sluggish lives to action.

In light of all of this, the question is not "Why are some people book-crazy?" but rather "Why aren't more people bookaholics?"

The proprietor of one of the bookstores in the mall told me last week that he had heard that only 15 percent of the American population now reads books.

I hope this is an erroneous figure. Only 15 percent of us ever crawl into bed early to be entertained by a spellbinding story? Only 15 percent of us care enough about truth to learn from the sages? Only 15 percent of our children know the joy of a rainy afternoon with the Hardy Boys or Nancy Drew? I pray it isn't so!

If it is, we will be impoverished for it. There is a slow discipline and a simmering joy in perusing a good book that cannot be matched by television, movies, or stereo. So I'll continue to feed my addiction and not feel too guilty about it. And I wouldn't be too upset if both of you develop severe bookaholism too.

Addictively yours,

SNOWFLAKES AND FINGERPRINTS

The last two weeks' letters on fascination and my book addiction have me thinking this morning about individualism. I'm reminded that each of us is a one-of-a-kind, never-to-be-repeated creation. As one of my favorite writers, Virginia Owens, puts it, "Infinite creativity demands infinite diversity. Such are the attributes of God. No duplicates, whether of snowflakes or fingerprints, come from the hand of God."[2]

One man's fascination is steam engines, another's is books. One woman likes weightlifting, another is turned on by embroidery. God never uses a copy machine to produce people! And what is important for each of us is to be true to who we are. The hardest job you will ever have is to be your own self, to live your true identity. The whole world will conspire against your individualism. It will confidently dictate to you what you should wear, how you should smell, where you should work, and how you should relate to other people. Our world, unfortunately, *does* use copy machines to produce its citizens.

I have come to see our willingness to be true to our self as a real part of our Christian faith. So often when we think of the will of God we think of specific items God wants us to do. We think of God's will as a checklist we are to discover and obey — where to go to college, who to marry, where to work, which church to attend, and other important matters.

I have no doubt that we should seek God's guidance when we're facing those decisions. But I also know that we need to think of God's will as more than specific items on a divine printout. I believe that God's will is that we be who He made us to be. I like the way Robert Capon says it: "The will of God is not a list of stops for us to make to pick up mouthwash, razor blades, and a pound of chopped chuck on the way home. It is his longing that we will take the risk of being nothing but ourselves, desperately in love."[3]

Translating that into our lives means this: We don't have to be loud and aggressive just because society rewards extroverts; we can be, even *must* be, quiet and sensitive if that is who we are. We don't have to get married, live in the suburbs, and join the corporate rat-race just because everyone else is doing it; we can find the style of life that fits us best, the style we sense we are being nudged toward by God. In short, we can find and be ourselves, and life will be a rich adventure. If we try to mimic the masses, we will strangle the very thing that nourishes the life within us — our peculiarity.

During most of your teenage years I have feared your nonconformity. Though I have kept my fears mostly secret, I have faithfully performed the parental ritual of "worrying about the kids": What if they rebel and become "hippies"? What if they want "punk rock" haircuts? What if they reject the Christian commitment upon which our family is built? I am an expert worrier, and I have worried much about your possible waywardness.

But I also know that as you grow older the danger you will face is the opposite one: You will be tempted to become one of the masses, to "go along to get along," to cast your lot with conformity. If you yield to that pressure, both you and your world will be poorer for it.

When I look at my peers, I see the awful, deadening effects of "fitting in." Most of my friends are nice, respectable, moral people, but the spark has gone out of their lives. They seem to be robots — going to work, attending church on Sundays, raising "happy" families. But the joy has somehow leaked out of their lives. Through the years, they have lost their sense of adventure.

Don't let the world squeeze you into its mold. Keep your peculiarity. Be obstinate in your individualism. That's the best advice I can give you for staying alive all your years. I hope both of you will always take the risk of being nothing but yourselves, desperately in love — in love with God, with people, with life.

And know this: I kind of like you just the way you are. Unusual, yes. Unique, for sure. Different even from your father, without question. But the pride of my life forever.

Peculiarly yours,

Dad

FINDING THE WILL
OF GOD

I sort of got in over my head in the last letter. Discussing the will of God is a precarious endeavor. Most pontifications on the subject, I think, are too confident and certain. Many people who diagram specific directions for finding God's will need a good dose of Isaiah 55:8: " 'My thoughts are not your thoughts, neither are your ways my ways,' says the Lord." But since I am seldom hesitant to wax eloquent on any subject, I will venture deeper into those waters and give you a few more reflections on the will of God. Hopefully we'll make it through without drowning!

One of the most helpful treatments on the subject I've seen comes from Howard E. Butt's book *The Velvet-Covered Brick*. He suggests seven ways that God guides us. I see these seven ways as clues to finding God's will, or, to use another analogy, as seven tributaries that lead to the big river of the will of God.

Here are the seven things he mentions in the book.

• *Scripture.* We don't have to wonder about much of God's will for our lives. Scripture makes it plain that God wants us to worship, pray, give freely, love people, be free from constant anxiety, and a host of other things.

A good place to start if we want to know God's will is to read His Word and take seriously its commands. But be forewarned: The Bible is easier read than done! We might be like Mark Twain and have to admit that it's not the parts of Scripture we *don't* understand that bother us but the parts of Scripture we *do* understand.

• *Self-love.* I used to have a foolproof formula for finding the will of God: Whatever I didn't want to do, whatever I dreaded and despised, was God's desire for me. But now I know that just the opposite is usually true: Whatever I love and enjoy is likely to be God's will for me. He whispers to me through my own gladness. Frederick Buechner once suggested that God's will is usually where our delight and the world's need intersect. That's as good a definition as we'll ever find. Listen to your heart, know what gives you joy, and you'll have a real clue about God's guidance.

• *Structure.* We live in a world of structure. Families, churches, businesses, schools, and governments are the building blocks of society. A part of finding the will of God is learning to submit to those who lead us in these various structures. I know that submission is not a popular idea these days. Aggression and assertion fit better in our world. But servanthood is, and always will be, the key to Christianity. We have to ask periodically "Who's in charge here?" and then submit to that authority.

· *Self-denial.* We must also trust other people. God sometimes takes on the voice of a spouse, a son or daughter, a friend, or even an enemy to prod us into His will. In other words, we don't have to grope for God's direction on our own. We can seek the counsel of other people and get a frame of reference beyond our own hunches. A real key to sensing God's will, I've discovered, is to have a few people you can be honest with, a few people who know you intimately and want the best for you. In bouncing thoughts and concerns off them, you can better hear the voice of God.

· *Simplification.* Take heart — you are not responsible for the whole world! You are responsible only for honing your own gifts and using them. A good question to ask when facing a decision is "Can anybody else do it?" As I mentioned in the previous epistle, we are all uniquely equipped for something. When we find our "thing" and zero in on it, we've taken a giant step toward knowing what our contribution to the world is to be.

· *Situations.* God often speaks through circumstances. As the calendar of our lives unfolds, we are confronted with specific situations that demand a response from us. If we look beneath those events, we may hear God saying something. Our misery may signal the need to change jobs. Our family woes may tell us to devote our attention there. Flunking math may indicate that God doesn't want us to be a mathematician. God doesn't often thunder edicts from heavenly places; He speaks quietly in the ordinary events of our lives. I love Buechner's description of what he calls the "alphabet of grace": "If there is a God who speaks anywhere, surely he speaks here: through waking up and working, through going away and coming back again, through people you read and books you meet, through falling asleep in the dark."[4]

· *Serenity.* There is an inexplicable inward witness that affirms us when we're on the right track. Some decisions just feel right. When we listen to our "insides" and choose the correct path, our reward is serenity. We know what the apostle Paul described as "the peace of God which passes all understanding." Remember this as you hunt for God's will: He is not the God of misery, but the God of peace.

To be perfectly honest with you, I have always been adept at seeing God's will *in retrospect*. I can look back on some past events and see the unmistakable fingerprints of God's hand. But at the time I was experiencing those events I felt like I was flying by the seat of my own breeches! I probed and prayed and finally stepped out without much evidence of divine instruction. I wish God would speak audibly or at least send an occasional telegram, but He hasn't so far, and I'm not holding my breath.

I do believe, though, that in mysterious and subtle ways God nudges us along, and that we should do everything possible to be aware of those nudges. I hope these seven ideas will help both of you as you seek to find your niche and contribute your special "thing." And if I can ever be a sounding board, you know I'm available.

Love,

Dad

THE ROLLER COASTER CLUB

I'm forming a club and thought you might be interested in joining. It'll be called The Roller Coaster Club, and membership will be open to anyone 16 or older who rides an emotional roller coaster. Anyone who has the capacity to soar with the eagles one day and grovel with grubworms the next is eligible.

For a five-dollar membership fee, you'll get a card certifying you as an official member and an invitation to our annual Roller Coaster Club Convention. At these an-

nual affairs, we will pool our misery and then share secrets for surviving the ups and downs of the ride. Sound enticing?

I fully expect to become a millionaire because of this idea. Though we roller coaster riders are usually quiet about our plight, I suspect our numbers are legion. At five bucks a head, I could become a wealthy man very quickly!

Of course there are some people in Christian circles who would call our fluctuating ride sin. These Christians believe that Christ calls us to continuous ecstasy, that any admission of "low days" is a telltale sign that we're backslidden. Some believe that the Christian life is a constant "high," void of any valleys.

But I disagree. I can think of dozens of faithful Christians who could become charter members of my Roller Coaster Club. I can even think of some biblical heroes who would be prime candidates for membership if they were alive today.

Elijah, for instance — bold and cocky one day but depressed and suicidal under a juniper tree the next. Or Jonah, preaching the good news of forgiveness to the Ninevites but then cursing his life under a shrunken gourd plant a short time later. Or David, strumming his harp in praise to God some days and wallowing in dark, dark depression on other days. Or Jeremiah, wishing he could run from his problems to some little wilderness motel. Or Hosea, feeling betrayed by his beloved Gomer. Or John the Baptist, wondering from a prison cell if Christ actually was the promised Messiah. Or Paul, fighting the losing battle with his sinful "self" and doing what he knew was wrong.

We roller coaster riders, you see, come from good stock! When someone tells me that the Christian Way is all smiles and goosebumps, I know he is either extremely blessed or extremely ignorant. My experience, at least, testifies to an up-and-down journey that knows both joy and staleness. And I take heart that so many other people of faith seem to have had a similar ride.

All of this is to remind you that God never promised us a tiptoe through the tulips. Sometimes we'll be down. Some days we may even wonder if God exists. But our relationship to Him, thank goodness, doesn't rest on our fickle feelings; it rests on *His* faithfulness to us.

What we actually get when we become a Christian is not an exemption from the roller coaster of ordinary human feelings and experiences. That would be nice, but it just isn't so. What we get is a Friend who promises to take all of those harrowing dips and turns with us. We get a Companion who promises to ride with us all the way and to hold us securely in His eternal grip. If we soar with eagles, He is there. But if we grovel with grubworms, He is there too.

Well, I got on my theological hobbyhorse, but now I need to get back to my original question: Can I enroll you in the Roller Coaster Club?

The President of
The Roller Coaster Club,

Dad

MARATHON MAN

As you know, I am in training for my first marathon. As soon as I finish writing these words of wisdom to you, I plan to lace up my running shoes and hit the road. My training schedule calls for a 15-mile run today. Why, you may have wondered, is the old man punishing himself like this? What would cause a sensible middle-aged man to run himself into the ground? I'm not exactly sure myself, but let me attempt to rationalize this running foolishness to you.

Frankly, my marathon hopes may have something to do with the "middle-age crazies." When a man's hairline starts to recede, his waistline expands, and his skin wrinkles — when he finally realizes he's never going to make it as a major league shortstop or an NFL quarterback — strange things start to happen.

Some men buy "with it" clothes to protest the relentless march of time. Some get a young mistress. Some quit a respectable job and move to the wilderness. Some sink into deep depression. But I handled the "crazies" a different way. I bought a pair of running shoes and started logging countless miles around the neighborhood. In light of the other options available to me, that's not so bad, is it?

I would like to believe, too, that my marathon hopes are somehow connected to my Christian commitment. I'm willing to concede that I may be trying in vain to outrun Father Time by putting in my miles, but I also think it is my responsibility as a Christian to stay in good shape physically. Faith, remember, has a physical side to it also; it doesn't just concern the soul.

In New Testament days there was a group called the Gnostics who denied the physical side of faith. The Gnostics were superspiritual people who made religion all soul and no body. They believed that anything material or physical was evil, and that only "spiritual" things had any validity. Naturally, they scoffed at the idea of the incarnation of Christ, for they just knew that God would never reveal Himself in literal flesh and blood. Much of the New Testament was written to counter the tenets of the Gnostics and to remind us that God is concerned about the whole man, not just his spiritual part.

When the apostle Paul wrote the church at Corinth, for example, he emphasized the fact that commitment to Christ included taking care of the body: "Do you not know that your body is a temple of the Holy Spirit within you, which you have from God? You are not your own; you were bought with a price. So glorify God in your body" (1 Corinthians 6:19,20).

Unfortunately, those ancient Gnostics have a modern counterpart. The notion still abounds that God is concerned only about our souls, that He's not concerned at all about our intellect or our bodies. But I want you to remember the Gnostic heresy and not succumb to this modern version of it. I'm convinced that jogging can be as spiritual as praying (I usually do both at the same time), and that staying abreast of the current world situation is as Christian as memorizing the books of the Bible. God is interested in the total person. Trying to confine His interest to only one part of us limits His lordship.

When I run, I don't feel as if I'm doing something "secular" (as opposed to "sacred"). I think I'm responding to God's lordship over my life. Certainly we must do those "spiritual things" — go to church, study Scripture, pray, give our money for ministry, and all the other necessary disciplines. But we must never section those things off and assume that they are God's primary concerns. I think He's concerned about *us*, about every nook and cranny of our lives. We must also read good books, be informed citizens, learn how to handle stress, watch what we eat, and get plenty of exercise. Those things are spiritual too.

The road beckons. The air has a nip to it this morning, but there's hardly a trace of wind. It's 50 degrees, I would guess, and clear — an ideal day for running. One more cup of this coffee and I'm off to battle the "middle-age crazies" and to do my duty to a life-encompassing God.

Just call me the Marathon Man.

Running the race,

Dad

SAVORING THE LITTLE THINGS

Last week a masked man wearing a wig scaled one of the skyscrapers in Houston. You probably read about it in the paper. With suction cups on his hands and feet, he slowly ascended the glass structure for over 12 hours. When he reached the sixty-eighth floor, he jumped. His parachute worked beautifully, and he landed safely on Lamar Street. Houston police officers greeted him there and carted him to jail. Bail for the building-climber was set at 20,000 dollars.

I thought of his exploits when I read an article in this morning's *Post*. The article was titled "Are You a Sensation Seeker?" Some people, the article said, thrive on danger and adventure; they live for sensation. One ecstatic "high" must be followed by another. The article insinuated that these devil-may-care sensation-seekers are the ones among us who really experience life. There was even a test to determine if the reader qualified as a sensation-seeker. I took the test eagerly — and failed miserably! I could honestly answer only one question in the affirmative: I *do* like spicy foods.

A pitiful image of self descended upon me. "Here is a boring man," a voice inside me whispered. "He has never climbed a building, parachuted from a plane, taken a trip around the world in a sailboat, or walked across America. He's even afraid of roller coasters! This man is definitely a deadhead!"

As much as I wanted to, I could not deny the charges. My idea of a good time is a soft bed, a stimulating book, and a hot cup of coffee. I get a thrill out of picking berries, listening to smooth harmony, and taking our family to get doughnuts. Given a choice between going to Astroworld or jogging three miles, I'll always choose the latter. And when it comes to worship, give me no drums or hugs or shouting. Just give me quiet and leave me alone.

But I protest the article's implication that I do not qualify as a sensation-seeker. I like sensations, and even seek sensations. It's just that I don't need to scale a building to get a lump in my throat. I can get that when I stand on the beach and look at miles and miles of ocean, or when I sit in my recliner at night and gaze at our twinkling Christmas tree.

Certainly we all want adventure in our lives. I have no quarrel with building-climbers, sky-divers, and stock-car-racers. They are but loud reminders that we all crave excitement and danger. Boredom is a killer, and the human spirit always resists it.

But don't ever underestimate the joy that can be found in the little things of life. Most days are going to be pretty routine for most of us. Even brave building-climbers don't scale skyscrapers every day. Most of life is pretty normal, routine stuff. Go to school, talk to friends, eat meals, listen to records, watch television, go to bed. The person who demands constant thrills will always be disillusioned by life.

That's why it is so important to savor the little things. Adventure can be found in the ordinary if we know how to look for it. We can build into every day some "pockets of joy" that keep life from growing stale. A book, a record, a cup of coffee and the sports page, a special friend, a trip to get an ice-cream cone, a stroll around the block to think and pray — these and a multitude of other treats can add flavor to our lives.

I believe the really contented people in our world are not the ones who have to climb buildings or party every night to get a thrill. The really contented people are the ones who get excited about a stamp collection or a telephone conversation with a friend. Those people — the ones who have learned to savor the little things — are the ones who experience the abundant life.

I hope both of you find excitement galore though I'd prefer that you not climb skyscrapers, or if you do, please don't tell me about it! Seek adventure. Flee boredom. Don't be afraid to risk.

But relish those ordinary things, too. If you learn to do that, you will never lack for "sensations." Build some of those "pockets of joy" into your routine, and run to them with regularity.

I'll close this letter and run to one now myself — the coffeepot is still half full, and I saved the comics as my reward for finishing this masterpiece.

The Daredevil,

Dad

THE NOT-SO-FASTBALL

I'm embarrassed. Humiliated. Dejected. Your unrestrained glee at my ineptness didn't help much either. Had I known I would fare so poorly, I never would have paid good money to display my fastball at the carnival booth last night. When I fired my first pitch at the target and the radar gun clocked it at 46 miles per hour I couldn't believe it. When my second pitch came in at 50, I suspected something was amiss. When my third and final effort registered a 51, I was crestfallen. If Nolan Ryan can throw a 100-mile-per-hour fastball, I thought I could surely

come in at about 75. But 51? And my arm is throbbing this morning from trying so hard!

As I reflect on what happened last night, I realize now that the carnival booth was rigged. The radar gun was wrong and recorded a false speed. You know how carnival booths are — stacked against the contestants. Those carnival folks have a limited number of teddy bears, so they told the gun to tell a lie. That's the most logical explanation for my 51-mile-per-hour fastball. After all, you both saw the pitch I fired. You heard it crack against the target. You saw it zip like a bullet through the air. Honestly, did that look like a 51-mile-per-hour fastball to you? No way!

Of course, there is the slight but more depressing possibility that I really did top out at 51. It is remotely possible that the radar gun was accurate and correctly recorded my not-so-fastball for the whole world to see. Did you know that a major league change-up is about 70 miles per hour? There is no pitch in any pitcher's repertoire that is effective at 51.

Years ago one pitcher tried a "blooper ball" that arched rainbowlike to the plate. As I recall, he only tried it a couple of times because the fans laughed so hard at him. But if I'm ever going to make it to the majors I'll have to make it as a "blooper ball" pitcher.

The remote possibility that I'm not gifted with a big-league arm underscores again what I was trying to say in the "Snowflakes and Fingerprints" letter. Some people can pitch, some can preach. Some can sing, some can sew. Some run races, some run big businesses. But each of us can do something well. The trick is to find that "something" and then do it to God's glory.

So, even if the radar gun told the truth, maybe I shouldn't grieve too much. I'll bet I can strum the guitar better than Nolan.

The Fireballer,

Dad

LAUGHTER REALLY IS GOOD MEDICINE

Did we ever talk about Norman Cousins' book *Anatomy of an Illness*? It seems to me we discussed it at the supper table one evening. But just in case you've forgotten our conversation, let me refresh your memory and remind you in this letter of the necessity of laughter in our lives.

The book details Cousins' recovery from a critical illness. He decided to take his recuperation into his own hands, and tried something medically heretical. He shunned ordinary treatment and opted instead for big doses of vitamins and regular times of laughter. Every day he had a pro-

jector brought into his room and watched funny movies. A surprising thing happened: He made remarkable progress! Tests were run "before laughter" and "after laughter," and they always showed a marked improvement following his gleeful sessions at the movies. Cousins is convinced that laughter literally releases a healing potion into our bodies and that it was a prime factor in his recovery.

Now I'm not advocating that you disregard all medical advice and turn to self-healing. Nor do I want you to throw away the aspirin in the medicine chest. But I do want you to remember the power of laughter. I tend to agree with Norman Cousins: I think laughter actually heals. Medical science will no doubt one day verify the old adage in Proverbs: "A cheerful heart is a good medicine, but a downcast spirit dries up the bones" (Proverbs 17:22).

One of the nicer things you've done for me through the years is give me reason to laugh. I have found great delight in watching you move from infancy to childhood to adolescence to almost-adulthood. You two have been my main source of merriment, my "funny movies." Even now I can recall some of the things you've said and done and some of the things we've done together, and I have to chuckle. My mind is crammed with hilarious memories. When you leave home, I may have to buy a projector and start watching classic comedies.

It bothers me that the Christian life is so often presented as a drab, somber march. We Christians are so serious! We act like our gospel is bad news instead of the best news ever unleashed into the world. I think it's time for Christians to start living the Good News, to act like forgiven, liberated adventurers. One of the great poets reportedly wrote in his journal, "Wonder of wonders! I have been to church today and am not depressed." I know the feeling, don't you?

I'm currently reading a book called *The 2000 Mile Turtle*. It's a funny, tongue-in-cheek book, and you can't read it without a grin. One line in the book bears remembering and repeating: "Next to love, laughter is the best answer to the universe."[5]

That's true. If you have love and laughter in your lives, you'll do fine. Whatever destiny hurls at you, you'll be able to survive and even triumph. Circumstances will never defeat you because you have found a potent one-two punch.

As I sit here at the kitchen table and think about my hopes for you, I offer you a simple two-step approach to life: Keep loving, and keep laughing!

Selah!

Dad

HOW TO PICK
A PREACHER

One of the things you will have to do when you leave "the nest" is choose a church. All these years you've not had that freedom because you've just tagged along with us. I hope when you get out on your own you'll be able to find a good community of faith that will both challenge you and give you opportunity to serve. Being in the right church is crucial to one's spiritual condition.

Churches vary: Some are electric with enthusiasm; some are as drab as ditchwater. You will never find a perfect church, but you can find one that needs you and fits your style.

A part of picking a church is picking a preacher. And they vary, too. You can't lump all preachers into one category any more than you can call all flowers identical. Every preacher is unique. One is authoritative and rules like a tyrant; another is mild-mannered and never goes to committee meetings. One shouts when he preaches; another reads matter-of-factly from a manuscript. You'll have to decide for yourself which type best suits your needs.

As an expert preacher-watcher, I want to give you some priceless gems of wisdom on how to pick a preacher. What you want to look for is a person free of most of the common ministers' maladies.

Medical science has now discovered a whole series of diseases unique to preachers. Here is a list of some of the more prevalent ministers' maladies and the symptoms of each disease.

• STATISTICOSIS. Measures the effectiveness of every event by how many people attend; constantly counts heads and announces totals to congregation; sinks into deep depression when crowds thin and statistics drop; also known as *numbermonia*.

• AUTHORITIS. Gets sermons from sermon books penned by other preachers; seldom has an original thought but thinks no one notices; occasionally drops the names of noted writers to give the illusion of intellectualism; also known as *plagiarosis*.

• HARDENING OF THE CATEGORIES. Tends to see everything as black and white; lumps people into rigid groups (conservative, liberal, fundamental, them, us); is fond of labels and stereotypes.

• SIMPLE SYNDROME. Reduces everything to simple formulas; is fond of three-point sermons, each beginning with the same letter; also called *formulitis*.

· FLEEBITIS. Moves to a new field of service every two or three years; hears God's call to a new work whenever 1) he runs out of old sermons, 2) dissension occurs, or 3) he's offered a higher salary. Also known as *Samsonite syndrome, newmonia,* and *roamatism.*

· HALOTOSIS. Strikes an angelic posture of perfection before the church; refuses to act like an ordinary human; face becomes frozen in a forced smile.

· JARGONITIS. Uses "catch words" frequently; is fond of phrases like "share a testimony," "get saved," "a Christian walk," "profession of faith," and "believe the Word," but doesn't explain their meaning; puts serious searchers to sleep.

· INSAMENIA. Congregation knows order of worship and sermon content before entering church building; preacher uses same phrases and tone of voice Sunday after Sunday; is often linked in deadly form with *jargonitis;* also called *predictabilliosis.*

If you can find a preacher free of all these illnesses, you have found a rarity. Listen to him attentively. Cultivate the relationship. And call me. I want to meet that preacher too.

Yours for telling it like it is,

STRANGE STRATEGY FOR SUCCESS

While browsing through a bookstore earlier this week, I noticed again how many books there are on success. The shelves were stuffed with treatises offering advice on how to be a successful human being. I have no doubt that those books sell, and sell big. We all want to make it in life, to be dubbed a success by other people.

Several months ago I read one of these success books myself. It promised to give me "attitudes and strategies for winning what *you* want in life." That sounded good to me, so I bought it (it was only a three-dollar paperback) and read it in a couple of days. I suppose I profited by it, but I also

felt uncomfortable with some of the book's counsel. As a Christian schooled in Scripture, I saw much of the book as conflicting with biblical advice on successful living. The book made me realize that society's way to success and Scripture's way to success are divergent roads.

The one biblical episode that came to my mind was Jesus' encounter with the rich young ruler. I think the underlying issue in that encounter was success. The man was young, rich, and moral — surely three of the key ingredients in the pie of success. And yet he was restless and searching for more. I think the rich young ruler came to Jesus because he had achieved all the prescribed steps in successful living and still felt like a failure. And I have a hunch there are thousands of rich, young, moral people in our society who find themselves in the same dilemma.

What Jesus told the young searcher gives us a good clue to what it takes to be successful: "If you would be perfect, go, sell what you possess and give to the poor, and you will have treasure in heaven; and come, follow me" (Matthew 19:21). Dissect that bit of counsel and you will find four distinct steps in building a successful life. Since these four principles are consistently undergirded by other New Testament teachings, I feel safe in offering you this plan of success. You will never see this strategy in the popular self-help manuals, so pay close attention. This is revolutionary stuff, suitable only for bold nonconformists!

Dethrone things. Christ first told the young man to get rid of his possessions. Before we throw stones at the ruler for being a selfish materialist, let's consider this frightening question: Would we sacrifice all our precious "goodies" to follow Christ? The most honest answer is: Probably not.

I think Jesus made this stringent request of the man because he had built his life on "things." The only way he would be ready for real discipleship was to destroy that foundation and start over. Like Nicodemus, he had to be born all over again and begin from square one.

Now that is radical advice! Our society teaches us that success is a matter of accumulating "goodies," not getting rid of them. Like the ruler, we measure our worth by the trinkets we possess. To think of living without cars, stereos, and microwaves is painful indeed! But those of us who believe in Christ's plan for success know that "things" don't give us what we crave. The more we get, the more we have to have. It's a vicious cycle that finally leads to disillusionment.

I'm not suggesting that you become penniless hermits. I'm not even planning to sell your stereos. But I do want you to remember that our possessions cannot satisfy our deepest yearning. Only God can.

Invest in people. Christ told the young man to take the money he received from selling his stuff and give it to the poor. The ruler was being asked to make a radical shift in his priorities — from acquisition to servanthood. Had Christ told him to invest in stocks, commodities, or real estate, I feel certain the man would have gladly complied. But Christ invited him to invest his substance in people, and he was not ready for that.

Consistently Jesus reminds us in the Gospels that people are life's best investment. After all, people are eternal. Stocks fall, commodities crumble, and real estate erodes into the sea. But the human soul lasts forever. Therefore He calls us to give our time and money to people.

Gamble on the unseen. What if Jesus had said to the young searcher, "Sell what you have, give the money to the poor, and you will have treasure in the First National Bank of Jerusalem"? Don't you think the man would have done this? But Christ asked him to gamble on the unseen, to risk his current fortune on some unnameable treasure in some unknown land called heaven. Who wants to run that kind of risk?

Christians do! We Christians have bet our lives on unseen realities. We may be the biggest fools in the history of mankind! We have committed our lives to a God we've never seen to guide us in ways we can't comprehend to a heaven we've never even glimpsed. But we take heart that the truest, deepest realities — love, hope, joy — can never be seen in a microscope or explained by a computer.

Follow Jesus. Christ's final summons to the searcher was "Come, follow me." He said that several times in the Gospels. He frequently invited people to join Him on the road, to assume His priorities, to live His kind of life. The final step in the successful life — after dethroning "things," investing in people, and gambling on the unseen — is to follow Jesus and live for Him. Without this crucial step we will always be groping for something that will satisfy our spiritual thirst.

You will no doubt read books like the ones I saw this week at the bookstore that will offer you guaranteed formulas for successful living. That's fine, but don't forget the rich young ruler. He stands as an eternal reminder to us that what the world calls success can still leave you searching for something better. I hope you'll both have the grit to give a try to Jesus' strange strategy for success!

Yours for the good life,

Dad

MARCUS ALLEN
AND LIFE

I watched Marcus Allen carry a football for the Los Angeles Raiders last Sunday on television, and I was intrigued by his effortless grace. He made it look so easy — like anybody with two legs could gain a hundred yards against the Cleveland Browns. He just seemed to glide along, merrily slithering by all those helmeted monsters trying to devour him. No sweat. No strain. Just smooth and easy.

Watching him run reminded me of watching Hank Aaron hit a baseball. I'm truly sorry that neither of you got

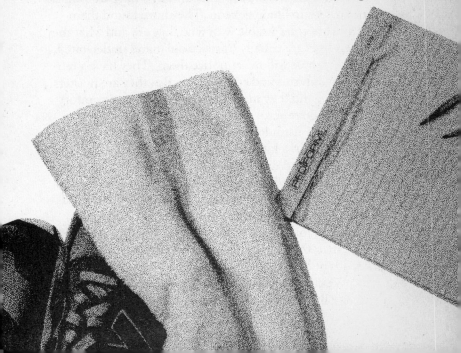

to see Hank in his prime. He made it look so easy to hit a baseball 400 feet. He would just nonchalantly snap his wrists, and the ball would zoom off his bat like a rocket.

The really good athletes make their sport look easy. Watch Chris Evert-Lloyd play tennis. Watch Lee Trevino hit a golf ball. Watch Joan Benoit run a marathon. They look like they're not even trying. Because they are so good at what they do, they give you the impression that anybody can coast along and win Wimbledon or the Masters or the Boston Marathon.

I've always admired athletes with that kind of skill. And I've noticed that their capacity for making hard things look easy is common among skilled people of all trades. Listen to a first-rate singer. Read a top-notch writer. Watch a craftsman build a cabinet or a seamstress sew a dress. The really good ones don't huff and puff or strain or try too hard. They just glide through their specialty and make it seem simple.

There are a few people around who have this knack when it comes to life in general. They have found themselves and are comfortable with who they are and what they do. Their lives are usually unspectacular and understated, and many people will never notice them. They have a tendency to avoid frills and commotion. But they are masters at living life, and they make you feel relaxed and comfortable in their presence.

Don't misunderstand: These experts at living didn't get there without a lot of work. Living is an art, a craft that demands time and discipline. Chris Evert-Lloyd got her smooth two-handed backhand only after hours and hours of practice and dozens of blisters. Lee Trevino developed his casual swing by "hustling" for years on municipal courses. And Joan Benoit didn't suddenly start breezing through marathons; she had to spend years running the back roads of Maine.

We can't expect to master the art of living overnight. We'll have to study our souls to see who we are, discipline our minds and bodies, and turn away from any activity that causes us to compromise. Living abundantly is tough business, and those who make it look easy have paid their dues.

But I hope you'll embark on — or continue on — this quest. And I hope you can find some models of genuine living who can inspire you. My last epistle, about the ruler and success, left me somewhat uneasy, because I know all of us need more than written principles of success if we are going to live abundantly. We need flesh-and-blood examples, too. If we are going to be truly successful, we need to know some real people who, by living the difference to which they have been called, encourage us to do the same. When it comes to learning about life, a person is worth a thousand principles. If you can find such a person, study him or her well. You'll learn some valuable lessons. If you can't find such a person, the next best thing is watching Marcus Allen carry a football.

Yours for a hard life
that looks easy,

WATCH OUT FOR GNATS AND MOLEHILLS

This letter was prompted by an embroidered plaque I saw this week. Stitched in red was this pointed prayer:

LORD, DELIVER ME FROM THE GNATS — I CAN HANDLE THE ELEPHANTS MYSELF.

The more I've thought about that prayer, the more I agree with its message. Gnats are more lethal than elephants. Molehills are more dangerous than mountains. The little irritations of life do more to sabotage our serenity than the big catastrophes.

Most of the time we can handle the major tragedies we face. Our bodies respond with a surge of adrenaline, our minds become alert to danger, and other people rush to our aid. After all, elephants and mountains are easy to detect! Though formidable, they at least give us warning of their presence.

It's the ants and molehills that send us into a tizzy. It's the trifling, nearly unnoticed irritations that ruin our day and sour our disposition. Because they are so "ordinary" and seemingly trivial, we don't arm ourselves for combat and, like Jericho before Joshua, we are defeated without even putting up a battle.

I want to warn you here and now of "the peril of the piddling." In fact, I want to go even further and point out some of the common irritations that can rain on our joy. At least, after reading these words of wisdom, maybe you can better recognize the enemy.

Here is an up-to-date list of a number of gnats that can make you miserable and molehills that can send you sprawling:

- Loose glasses that keep slipping down on your nose.
- A wet morning newspaper.
- Dogs that delight in scattering your trash all over the lawn.
- Christians that turn Christ's way into a get-rich-quick scheme for success.
- People who give easy, flippant answers to hard, sacred questions.
- Socks with no elastic.
- The telephone ringing just as you're drifting off to sleep.
- A prank caller in the middle of the night.
- A pushy, never-take-no-for-an-answer salesperson.
- A mailbox full of junk mail and bills.
- Several summer days without air conditioning.
- A dripping faucet that gets louder and louder the harder you try to sleep.

- A stubborn headache that aspirin won't cure.
- A person whose favorite topic of conversation is himself.
- A car that won't start when you need to be somewhere important *now*.
- Writing a hot check even though your calculations showed you still had $7.52 in your account.
- People who keep long lists of irritations.

Now that I look back over that inventory, I realize that these are the things that perturb *me*. Perhaps your enemy has a different face. But hang on to this letter anyway. As you get older, you may find that you are irritated by the same things I am.

Here's the one thing I've learned, though, in a lifetime of doing battle with pygmy problems, and the one thing I want you to get from this letter: Laughter kills gnats, and molehills shrink when doused with humor.

Patiently yours,

STAYING POWER

Peter DeVries, the humorous novelist, once said, "I love being a writer. It's the paperwork I can't stand." I know the feeling. There's nothing harder than gluing your breeches to a chair to write something, especially if you suspect that your literary effort will never be published. It's tough to polish a piece of writing when you suspect that it's for self-edification only.

But there's something to say for plain old dogged tenacity — in writing and in life. On the heels of my gnats and molehills piece, I want to write this week in praise of persistence.

When baseball blooms again next spring, ageless
Pete Rose will once more be in the headlines. Pete is getting
old now and never has had the finest physical tools in the
majors. He is not too strong or too big or too fast, and his
arm is not great. But he'll march right into the Hall of Fame
when he retires because he hustled and never thought of
quitting. Pete made it big because he had good talent and
great determination. He stands as a symbol of success
through sweat. He reminds us that tenacity is usually a prerequisite to accomplishment.

In a short while, both of you will graduate from high
school. We will celebrate that occasion in grand style, I'm
sure, and all our merriment will really be in honor of your
perseverance. For 13 years counting kindergarten, you've
gone to school, taken tests, done homework, and performed
all the other duties required by the educational system.
Your graduation will be a well-deserved recognition of the
strength you had to plod gamely to the finish line.

This brings me, strangely enough, to some things
Jesus said about life. He told once of a builder who began
construction of a tower but ran out of money before he got
it erected. He told of a king who went to battle but failed to
recruit enough soldiers to stand a chance for victory. He
told of four kinds of soil — each implanted with a seed, but
only one bringing forth any fruit. He told of some people
who boasted of fine achievement but whose commitment
to Him was more talk than action. He said that anyone who
wanted to follow Him had better be ready to put his hand
to the plow and never look back. Really, stick-to-itiveness
was a major emphasis in His teaching.

And, of course, He practiced what He preached. Of
all the qualities of Jesus' life — compassion, sensitivity, in-
telligence, courage, and all the rest — here's one we often
overlook: His steadfastness. He never ran from conflict,
and He never shirked His calling. He even refused to flee
from the horror of the cross. He Himself put His hand to
the plow and never looked back. When the going got hard,

He never flinched. And His staying power purchased our pardon.

The mood of our day seems to fly in the face of all of this. The "if it feels good, do it" mentality of the age has as its natural corollary "if it doesn't feel good, quit." When studies get arduous and rob you of pleasure, drop out of school. When the marriage isn't going well, file for divorce. When the job gets tedious, look for new employment. When God doesn't respond as you wish, give up on Him and live for self. Staying power is in short supply these days and will likely get scarcer in the days ahead.

So on this Saturday morning I'm applauding tenacity. Three cheers for all who, even in the midst of hardship, "walk and do not faint."

Yours for the long haul,

BOSSY AND
THE DOVE SHIRT

I awakened this morning at six as usual. I know you have a hard time comprehending why any sane person would get up at six on Saturday. All I can say in my defense is that my internal clock is no discerner of days. It can't tell Saturday from Monday and feels obliged to shake me into consciousness with daily regularity.

But I got up troubled and perplexed because I didn't have any profound words of wisdom to lay on you this morning. Divine inspiration never came this week, and my mind has been stewing in its own uncreative juices.

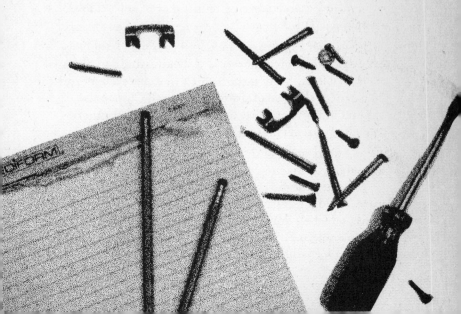

So I put on the coffee and started rustling through the morning paper. I got no further than page 4 in the front section when two items, adjacent to each other, caught my attention. I read both with interest, and the idea for this epistle suddenly started taking shape. Inspiration just in the nick of time! Actually, I'm not sure I can say that this idea is heaven-sent, but I do think it bears considering. Let me tell you of the two items in the paper and then try to make some sensible connection between them.

Item one: A brief, human interest article on a deer-hunting episode. It seems that the deer-hunters in upper New York are a bit enthusiastic and wild. One wise farmer, having seen their unrestrained fervor before, took steps to protect his livestock. On both sides of one of his milk cows, for example, he painted COW in large letters. Surely, he must have thought, Bossy is safe now from the hunters. But, alas, some crazy marksman mistook Bossy for a fleet deer and felled her with one shot.

One moral of that story: Signs just don't mean much anymore.

Item two: An ad for Christian sportswear. A handsome young man is wearing tennis shorts and a "Dove" sport shirt. The copy reads:

See ya later alligator—I'm in love with the Dove! Dove Sportswear has what the world is looking for, and we're excited! Clean, fashion sport shirts in today's colors and fabrics with the logo of distinction for all Christians . . . .

Send in for your shirts today and tell some brothers, too! Get bold, get blessed, get Dove!

One moral of that ad: It's important to wear a sign identifying yourself as a Christian.

Now for the connection. I think we Christians can learn a valuable lesson from poor Bossy. We can learn that signs and labels don't do much convincing anymore. Surely that distraught farmer knows now that if a man can't recognize unadorned Bossy as a full-fledged member of the cow family just as she is, no sign in the world will make any difference. And if people can't recognize us as Christians in a plain, unlabeled sport shirt, plastering a dove on the pocket won't help at all.

You see, we can erect our blinking neon signs on the front lawns of our churches, but no one should believe we're the church until we adopt the same goals that Jesus had. We can stick bumper stickers all over our cars and implore people to honk, repent, or love, but no one should believe our witness until they hear us talk and see us walk. I suppose we could even emblazon CHRISTIAN on our clothes and advertise our faith in bold fashion, but no one should really believe that sign until they catch a glimpse of Jesus underneath our fancy garb.

We don't need flashier signs, gaudier bumper stickers, or more impressive religious garments to be better witnesses for Christ. We need to live simple, genuine lives and believe that Jesus really does make a difference. Until we can do that and believe that, our trappings are a waste of money and a cover-up of the painful truth.

Bossy did more for us in her death than she ever could have in her life.

Love,

Dad

THE HANDWRITING ANALYSIS

Already I can see some themes developing in my correspondence to you. I notice, for instance, that I keep returning to the theme of individuality. In several previous letters I've encouraged you to discover and be true to your real self. And I'm sure that in the epistles to come I'll strike that chord some more.

Self-discovery is a never-ending process. Even at my advanced age I am still learning new things about myself and uncovering personal peculiarities I never knew existed. So don't think self-discovery is an exercise only for high

school students. I have a hunch that, if we're alert and sensitive enough, we'll be finding out about our true self on our deathbed.

While struggling through a people-infested shopping mall recently, I stumbled upon a rare opportunity to discover something about my real identity. There before me in the mall was a small computer, ready to analyze my handwriting for a small fee. Always eager to uncover my hidden self, I paid my money, signed my name on a small card, and fed my signature into that electronic brain for examination.

In a few moments the computer completed its work and spit out a slip of paper with the pertinent data on my identity. The results were rather shocking.

1. *You are an extrovert in every sense.* ("Who, me? You've got to be kidding! I'm a writer, a dreamer, a seeker of solitude. No one has ever accused me of being the life of the party.")

2. *You are attractive to the opposite sex.* ("Maybe this computer is smarter than I think. At least it knows one thing about me.")

3. *You love luxury and extravagance.* ("Not me! I'm no sinful materialist. For years I've preached the virtues of the simple life. I drive an old car and never read the fashion page.")

4. *You have a tendency to talk too much.* ("Come on, now! I'm the listener, the astute counselor, the one who always gives the other person the privilege of unloading a burden.")

5. *You are honest with yourself and others.* ("I knew this machine wasn't a total sham. Honesty is certainly one of my trademarks.")

What do you think? Does that computer's analysis of my handwriting seem anywhere near accurate to you? After reading that slip of paper, I decided that either that machine is a moneymaking gimmick or that I don't know myself as well as I thought. I suspect I do still have some

things to learn about my true identity, but the search for it
promises to be an eventful one.

Won't you join me in trying to find your true self
too? The hunt will be a fun adventure, and the eventual
prize is a life of joyful integrity. But remember this one
thing as you look: Avoid handwriting computers like the
plague. They may say something bad about you.

Your extroverted,
handsome, extravagant,
talkative, honest mentor,

Dad

DEALING WITH DOUBT

When I was a sophomore in college, I went through an awful time of doubting my salvation. I had made my commitment to Christ as a young boy but began to wonder, as a sophisticated collegian, if I really knew what I was doing when I made that decision. After all, how much can a seven-year-old understand about the Christian Way?

I was miserable for weeks. I remember sitting with friends at the Astrodome watching an Oiler-Cowboy football game and being overcome with depression. How could I enjoy football without the assurance that I was right with

God? I couldn't enter into that festivity at all because I was so mired in the gloom of doubt.

It was a newspaper article by Ruth Graham, Billy's wife, that finally freed me from my misery. She was responding to a question about assurance of salvation and said just what I needed to hear. To this day I maintain that her brief article was actually a telegram from heaven.

She said she couldn't remember the exact moment of her conversion but that she knew she had a relationship with God through Christ. She said that just because you can't remember your birthday doesn't mean you weren't born, and just because you can't pinpoint the precise moment of your conversion doesn't mean you aren't saved. She said to focus on the *now*, to look at your relationship to Christ *now* and not get too hung up on what happened years ago.

That was music to my doubting ears. I knew that Christ was important to me and that I wanted to live for Him. I knew I had a relationship with Him, but I was so concerned about my boyhood experience that I let the past dictate uncertainty to the present. In looking so intently *behind* me, I failed to see the joy of relationship *within* me. Anyway, since that heavenly telegram I've never doubted my salvation again.

This doesn't mean, however, that I never doubted again. In truth, that struggle for assurance seemed to launch me on a life of searching and discovering. I've asked questions about the Bible, prayer, the institutional church, the will of God, evil and suffering, and other theological concerns. Like Jacob at Peniel, I have wrestled with God and become wiser for it.

What I have learned about doubt from those tussles can be summed up in three sentences:

First, doubts are inevitable. Frederick Buechner, in his book *Wishful Thinking*, writes, "Whether your faith is that there is a God or that there is not a God, if you don't have doubts you are either kidding yourself or asleep."[6] The

Christian Way, remember, is a way of faith. If we walked by sight, we would have all the answers and never have any doubts. But living by faith means that we trust God even though we don't completely comprehend Him. Buechner is right: We're either deluded or asleep if we think we have all the pieces to the puzzle.

Second, doubts help us grow. We usually think of doubt as demonic, but I have come to see doubt as a tool that God uses to push us into deeper, more honest faith. I love the way Buechner puts it: "Doubts are the ants in the pants of faith. They keep it awake and moving."[7] Don't see your doubts as obstacles to growth but as opportunities for growth.

Third, work through your doubts — don't avoid them. Untended doubt ferments into disillusionment. I don't think God wants us to wallow in uncertainty or to live in the kind of gloom I experienced that night in the Astrodome. But I also don't think He wants us to ignore our questions or to stifle our honest curiosity. Unless we're willing to face our doubts, our Christianity will always be on a flimsy philosophical foundation. I think we need to pose our questions, and then dig like crazy for good answers. Eventually we'll come out of the tussle with a sturdier faith.

When you were younger, I often wanted to protect you from a variety of childhood hazards — squabbling with other kids, spilling milk on the carpet, falling off a bicycle, doing poorly on school tests, striking out in the big game, etc. But gradually I learned to step back and let you live your own lives, to allow you to face those hazards and learn from them. Had I removed them or always rescued you from sticky situations, I would have stunted your emotional growth.

I feel something of that same tension even yet. I want life to be smooth sailing for you, for you to feel God always near, and for your faith in Him to be strong. Part of me hopes that you never have to spend sleepless nights wrestling with truth. I sort of wish the ants of doubt would leave you alone! But I know you'll never mature spiritually without some honest struggle, and I just pray that when those tussles come you'll be able to emerge from them with an even stronger commitment.

Just keep this in mind: We'll never have all the answers we want. Life is not an intellectual puzzle waiting to be figured out; it is an adventure waiting to be lived. Our challenge is to muster all the faith we have and to live that adventure one day at a time.

Well, I wanted to write this epistle on dealing with doubt just in case it ever sneaks up on you and tries to steal your joy. You two have always been great adventurers, and I imagine you'll continue to be in the years ahead.

In fact, that's one thing I don't doubt at all!

With gratitude even for ants,

EXPERIENCING THE TRINITY

Since I tackled the subject of doubt in last Saturday's treatise, I might as well take on, this week, one of the most confusing doctrines in Christian theology. This one doctrine has sent many sincere people into doubt and disbelief. Let me pontificate this morning on the subject of the Trinity.

That God could be three Persons in one is, of course, an offense to our logic. There is no mathematical way that three can be one. That rattles against our reason, and well it should. But before I make a feeble attempt to make sense of the Trinity, let me say that the enigma built

into the doctrine does serve a purpose: It reminds us that God defies our rational explanations, that He is bigger than our human attempts to define Him. The idea of God as three-in-one underscores the fact that He is *God* and far beyond our finite formulations. Aren't you glad God can't be explained on a computer printout or figured out like an algebraic equation?

Let me try, though, to shed a little light on the concept of the Trinity. I think the idea of God as three-in-one was an experience long before it was a doctrine. The Trinity is the way man has encountered God in life.

Most explanations simply cannot capture experiences. Words are just too fragile to carry the heavy freight of human feeling. For example, one dictionary defines a kiss as "a compression of the closed cavity of the mouth by the cheeks giving a slight sound when the rounded contact of the lips with one another is broken." That doesn't quite get it, does it? The experience far surpasses the explanation!

The same is true when we try to explain God. Our experience with God far surpasses our doctrinal attempts to describe that experience. But we must try, and the doctrine of the Trinity is our way of picturing how God has revealed Himself to humanity.

He has come to us as Father, as *One above us*. We believe He is the Creator and Sustainer of the world. Like the potter above the clay, the architect looking down on the blueprints, or the proud father gloating over the bundle in the crib, God oversees His creation. When we call Him Father, we are recognizing His lordship over the universe, His capacity to be above and beyond us.

He has come to us, too, as Son, as *One behind us*. We believe He came in tangible, human flesh to redeem us. "The Word became flesh and dwelt among us," John exulted in his Gospel. Christians assert that in the Person of Jesus of Nazareth God became one of us. When we call Him Son, we are acknowledging God's entrance into human history as a man and His willingness to become one with His creation.

He has come to us, thirdly, as Spirit, as *One beside us*. We believe that God is still alive and well and rummaging around in our hearts. When we see His creation, we call Him Father. When we experience His redemption, we call Him Son. But when we try to express His current activity in our lives, we call Him Spirit. When we speak of the third Person of the Trinity, we are acknowledging the power of God in our lives *today*.

There you have it — the Trinity in all His functional glory! God the Father: our Creator and Sustainer. God the Son: our Kinsman and Redeemer. God the Spirit: our Friend and Guide.

Does that help? I hope so. But even if all of this is as clear as mud, here's the one truth I hope you'll remember: The Trinity is not something you explain; it is Someone you experience.

The resident theologian,

CHRISTIANITY IN A CAPSULE

As you both know, when mechanical ability was handed out, I was "in absentia." Fixing things has never been my forte. In fact, if I want to send my blood pressure soaring, all I have to do is start tinkering with the car or the television or a drippy faucet. My ineptness inevitably frustrates me, and I end up doing damage to both the item needing repair and my health.

Last night, for instance, I tried to put together the barbecue grill we just bought. Talk about an exercise in futility! In this case I never got past the printed instructions

to actually begin construction. Let me give you a direct quote from the instruction booklet (which, by the way, promised "easy assembly in less than an hour"):

1. Take the notched leg (#14) and slide onto bottom of grill bowl (#2). Using four ¼-inch screws, fasten leg to bowl, making sure lock-washers are in place and wing-nuts are tight. Slide leg to rear of bowl until notch catches on back panel. If leg is uneven, tap with hammer until bowl is level.

Am I just dumb, or is that Swahili? I read that one step ten times and suddenly got very interested in a television program! My passion for a barbecue grill was drowned in a sea of confusing information.

Have you ever felt that way — not about mechanical things but about spiritual matters? I sometimes get the feeling that we are drowning in a sea of baffling spiritual information. Every denomination has a different theology. Every radio preacher offers different counsel. Every book prescribes a different recipe for abundant living. Who are we to believe? How can we sort through this gigantic pile of spirituality to find something that will really nourish us and lead us to God? Which of these complicated instructions will enable us to build a house on a solid foundation?

One Scripture I turn to whenever confusion sets in is Matthew 22:37-40. For me, this passage is Christianity in a capsule. One of the Pharisees (who were experts at making things complicated) asked Jesus to pinpoint the greatest commandment. His question was really a trick, designed to pin Jesus down. How could anybody sift through all the Old Testament commandments and pick out just one as supreme?

But Jesus was up to the challenge, and in answering the man He gave us a crystallized, condensed version of the Christian faith. To all who ever get dizzy from all the advice tossed around these days, here's a concise, four-verse commentary on what it means to be a Christian:

You shall love the Lord your God with all your
heart, and with all your soul, and with all your
mind. This is the great and first commandment.
And a second is like it, You shall love your neighbor
as yourself. On these two commandments depend
all the law and the prophets.

Isn't that easy to understand? You don't need an
advanced degree in theology to comprehend that! Our
charter is to love. We are to love God with our whole being
and to love others as we love ourselves. On those two
pivotal commandments, Christ said, hang all the Old Testament law and prophets. When boiled down to its essence,
the Christian way is the way of love.

Of course, that's easier to say than to do! Knowing
that we are to love God and others and actually pulling it
off are two very different things. But at least these verses
clarify our quest. At least now we know the heartbeat of our
calling as Christians. We don't have to get sidetracked by
spiritual sideshows. Now we know: The center-ring attrac-
tion of the Christian faith is love.

When you get befuddled by the varied and mystify-
ing sounds around you, remember what Jesus said about
the great commandment. Then turn off the radio. Close
the book. Stop the debate. And read again His answer to
the Pharisee. I hope it will help your confusion as much as
it has helped mine.

Yours for a life of love,

Dad

A FEW THINGS
I'D LIKE TO HEAR

This morning's sports page had another story about a dissatisfied superstar. It seems he only makes a half-million dollars a year as a running back and feels grossly underpaid. Other running backs are making more, he argues, and, besides, he risks life and limb every time he steps on the field. Team owners are not so sure he has been mistreated and aren't knuckling under to his demands. It looks like it could be a long and heated dispute!

That article got me to thinking about some of the things I'd like to hear or read this year. I started dreaming impossible dreams and musing about unlikely proclamations. Just once I'd like to hear somebody say:

• The team is willing to pay me a million bucks a year, but I'm not worth that much money. No football player

is. Sure I had a great season. I never dreamed I'd rush for 2000 yards and that we'd win the Super Bowl. But how can I justify a million dollars a year when my daughter's kindergarten teacher makes 18,000 dollars?

· If elected president of this country, I'll do my best. I'll be honest and serve with compassion. But, frankly, the bureaucratic wheels of big government have been turning for a long time. I'll be lucky to get very much accomplished. I won't be able to balance the budget, reduce taxes, prevent foreign wars, or simplify your income tax form. But please vote for me anyway.

· I've been an editor at this same publishing house for 20 years, but this year I'm taking a different approach. I'm going to quit accepting shoddy, sensational books that sell big to gullible people. No, this year I'm looking for finely crafted books that explore the truth. Even though they probably won't sell millions of copies, really good books will be our priority.

· Honey, the reason our marriage is falling apart is that I've been selfish and insensitive to you. My tendency is to blame you for all our problems, but I see now that I'm at fault. Please forgive me.

· Yes, sir, the ad you got in the mail is legitimate. After you have taken a 30-minute tour of our resort, we'll give you a new microwave, a color television, and a check for 500 dollars. Thanks for coming to see us.

· We appreciate our faithful listeners who tune in each week. Pray for our ministry, but please don't send money. Your gifts last year far exceeded our expectations. We were even able to share our blessings with hungry people in Bangladesh.

I'm not holding my breath.

The Daydreamer,

Dad

SILENCE AND THE TROOPS IN PROVOLONE

One of the things I value most about these coffeepot sessions is the time of silence they afford me. After sipping a couple of cups of coffee and reading the paper, I let Critter in from the garage, and the two of us bask in genial solitude. As I write these very words, she is nestled in my lap, and the only sound in the room is her contented purring.

Silence is therapeutic, and I hope you'll grow to love it as much as I do. Maybe I'm just getting old, or maybe the frantic pace of our routine makes me appreciate silence as never before. Or maybe I've been exposed to too much loud

music through the years! (We've had a few discussions about that, haven't we?) But, for whatever reason, I love moments of quiet and seek them out whenever possible.

These moments of solitude enable me to reflect on who I am and where I'm going, to get in touch with God, to live life from a stance of tranquility instead of frenzy (sometimes!). Without these periods of silent reflection, I honestly believe I'd be a nervous wreck!

I thought about the value of silence last night as I was watching television. I watched two programs, and the contrast between them boldly underscored for me the benefit of silence.

The first one I watched was a *"bloopers-and-blunders"* program that showed people in a variety of embarrassing goofs. One segment had the host of the show posing as a reporter and asking people on the street this question: "Should we pull our troops out of Provolone? What do you think?"

Well, the question engendered a lot of opinion. One man said, "I think we should send *more* troops in there." Another said, "The President should make those kinds of decisions." A young woman responded, "Yes, we should remove all our troops from Provolone immediately." One honest fellow answered, "I don't even know where that is."

Neither did I, but, as it turned out, Provolone is a kind of cheese! The question was a trick, designed to see if people would admit their ignorance. Obviously, most wouldn't. It's better to be a dishonest know-it-all, I suppose, than an honest dummy.

We chirp answers like chickadees because we cannot bear to have other people know of our ignorance. And our noisy "knowledge" also allows us to escape those difficult truths which we can learn only in silence. Only in silence do we touch God. Only in silence do we get to know ourselves. Only in silence can we order our lives efficiently. Only in silence do we learn of the sins we need to confess.

Only with silence can we answer honestly the question about our military involvement in Provolone!

The other program I watched was a documentary on Thomas Merton, the Catholic monk who lived in silence in a Kentucky monastery. The show focused on Merton's life there with his silent brothers — their work, worship, discipline, and simplicity. What a stark contrast! Some human beings lived in total silence in monastic life; others glibly blabbed answers to a nonsensical question.

I realized after watching the Merton show that I'm not ready for complete silence. I'm too accustomed to the noise of the world and too immersed in the pace of suburbia. Have no fear — I will not enter a monastery anytime soon! But I do confess that I would rather be in constant solitude than to have to live every day with loud experts on the military situation in Provolone.

Sometimes, for the sake of your own sanity — hush!

Yours for the quiet life,

CYNICISM ABOUT CYNICISM

It seems to me that cynicism is the dominant mood in our society. Everywhere you turn, someone is sounding a note of pessimistic "realism" designed to shatter our optimistic illusions. Just about the time you think you've found a silver lining, someone somewhere will remind you that an ominous cloud surrounds it.

Television, we are told, is a demonic tool for destroying morality. Politics, the popular mood says, is a nasty game played by con artists and bureaucrats. Food is no longer viewed as a tasty gift from God; now, the researchers inform us, much of what we eat contains cancer-producing ingredients. Big business, we all know now, is out to get us. The institutional church, too, is just a business trying to

manipulate people for selfish gain. And we all know that most people can't be trusted, for everybody is "looking out for number one."

The list could go on and on, but you get my point. Cynicism, negativism, and distrust are deeply engrained within us. We have become a nation (world?) noted for its capacity to find a corner of darkness in the brightest of rooms. No matter how wide and shiny the silver lining is, we have all been conditioned to look instead for the raincloud.

Make no mistake: The cynic has his place. We do need a few folks to look for clouds and to tell us when we're too naively optimistic. After all, television *can* be harmful; some politicans *are* crooked; some food *is* dangerous; some businesses *are* out to get us; some churches *are* manipulative; and some people *can't be* trusted.

But too much cynicism breeds depression and suspicion. Too much negative thinking snuffs out any chance for happiness and optimism. I think it is about time for our mood to swing back the other way. It is time once again to concentrate on silver linings and quit hunting for clouds. It is time, as naive and outdated as it sounds, to accentuate the positive.

So — with you and Critter as my witnesses — I hereby make a promise. Today I'm going to shun criticism. Just for today I'm going to be a positive person and be thankful for all those little things that I ordinarily take for granted. Just for today I'm not going to throw stones at any of my favorite targets. Just for today I'm going to live a life of joyful gratitude.

Who knows? I may be just a product of our age myself. But this much I know: I'm growing a bit cynical about all of our cynicism!

The Optimist,

Dad

THE SONG
SAYS IT ALL

Thought you might be interested in the progress
of last week's vow of optimism. For a solid week I've
avoided those cynical thoughts that usually rain on my joy.
I even watched a rock video on television Tuesday night
without losing my cool or declaring that the whole world is
demonic!

I have actually done a pretty fair job, I think, of
practicing what I preached in the last epistle. As you both
know, I have a great gift for throwing verbal stones at a few
of my pet peeves. Cynicism is no stranger to my soul. But

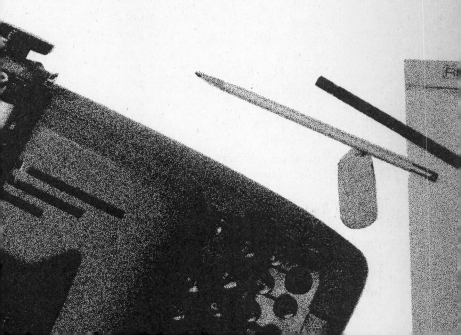

this past week, with my words of wisdom to you (us) fresh on my mind, I've been able to avoid negativism and concentrate on some blessings I frequently overlook.

There is a country song on the radio that says, "All the best things in life are free." That line has been around for years now and has pretty well lost its zing. But the more I've thought about it, the more I tend to think the old cliche is true. The best things in life, the biggest blessings we'll ever receive, cost nothing.

Unfortunately, my checkbook register doesn't seem to agree. In recent weeks the blue Malibu conked out and had to be repaired. The water heater quit heating. The dishwasher quit washing. The electric bill was exorbitant. All those things necessitated monetary expenditures. If the best things in life are free, why do I keep writing all these checks?

But then I think about those things that really make life worth living, and the old cliche does ring true. For example, here's my own tally for yesterday:

Ability to run through the neighborhood $0.00
Kiss at the front door $0.00
Theological ruminations with
   a kindred spirit $0.00
Talking to God about life $0.00
Letter in praise of one of my
   books $0.00
Chatter of little children on
   school playground $0.00
Basketball game on driveway $0.00
Leaves shining crimson and
   gold $0.00
Smell of chicken on barbecue
   grill $0.00
Frosty nighttime breeze and
   sparkling stars $0.00
Picking the guitar before bed $0.00
Instant sleep, free of worry
   and hassle $0.00

Add up all those delights and you get a big fat zero. Oh, I know a certain amount of money is needed to experience some of those treasures. We did have to pay to put up a basketball goal several years ago; I did have to pay the pawn shop guy a few bucks for my old guitar; and the sleep came easy because of the soft bed your mother and I got when we were first married. But basically the things that made yesterday so enjoyable had no price tag. They are available to anyone with the desire to experience them. The Don Williams country song says it all: "The best things in life are free."

In truth, we could survive without cars, dish-washers, water heaters, and electricity if we had to. Let's hope we never have to, but we *could* do it. We could not survive, however, without some of those gratis gifts that we get daily.

In light of all of this, the only sensible response to life is one of gratitude. Most of life is a gift, and it only seems proper to thank the Giver.

With gratitude,

Dad

WHEN THE CAMERA IS OFF

Last Saturday morning, after writing at the coffeepot, I hotfooted it to Galveston to run in the "Shrimp Run." I mentioned the race to you this week but forgot to share one episode in the race that I now see as a helpful parable. Let me relate the incident to you in this epistle and then try to extract a moral from it.

As I told you, I was entered in the five-mile race (we had a choice between two-mile, five-mile, or ten-mile distances). As with all the runs I'm in, I harbored no notions

of winning. I simply wanted to finish in a reasonably good time and then claim another colorful T-shirt for my collection.

The gun sounded promptly at 9 A.M., and several hundred of us took off down the seawall — some with intense abandon and others like myself with a noncompetitive shuffle. This was my third "Shrimp Run," and I plan to make it an annual event because it suits so perfectly my philosophy of running. My expressed goal in running is to always run slow enough to enjoy the scenery, and the awesome sight of the ocean sparkling in the morning sunlight makes this particular race ideal for me. I'm a confirmed ambler, a back-of-the-pack lollygagger who notices pennies on the pavement, flowers in the yard, and, in this case, waves caressing the beach.

Early in the race, though, my sightseeing was interrupted by a little boy — probably eight or nine years old — running along beside me. Suddenly his face lit up with a big smile and he broke into a sprint. I wondered about his surge of speed until I noticed a car on the road beside us with a camera protruding from one window. Someone — probably the boy's parents — was capturing this moment on film. The camera looked to be the kind used with VCR's, and for about 30 seconds it was focused on the speedy, smiling future-Olympian.

I noticed, though, that when the car moved on ahead and the camera vanished, the boy wilted like a flower in the desert. His confident grin became grim resolve, and his pace slowed to a fast walk. Even I passed him! As long as the camera was on, he ran like a midget Alberto Salazar. I have a feeling, in fact, that if the photographer had stayed with him through the whole race the kid might have set some kind of record. But, out of the limelight, he became a normal eight-year-old trying to survive a long ordeal.

Isn't that the way we run life's race, too? We perform like champs when others are watching, when someone is around to applaud our performance. But in secret, when no one is watching, our performance flounders, our piety fizzles, our morality nosedives. That little boy in the "Shrimp Run" is a parable of the way we live: pretty good on camera, pretty lousy when no one is looking.

Perhaps we need an occasional refresher course on Jesus' advice in Matthew 6. When we give our money to the needy, He counsels, we should give in secret and not even let our left hand know what our right hand is doing. When we pray, He says, we should head for the closet and speak to an audience of One. And when we fast, He instructs, we should do it in such a way that only God knows of our devotion. Whether giving, praying, or fasting, we are to avoid public notice and be faithful *in private*. In other words, the real test of our Christianity is how well we run *when the camera is off* !

Eric Hoffer, the longshoreman-philosopher, once wrote, "I have always equated individual as well as social health with the ability to perform well at room temperature."[8] If I understand Christ at all, I think He is saying that our faith can also be gauged that way. How well we live our faith at room temperature — when the camera is off and the spectators have gone home — is the true measure of our relationship to Him.

Have a good week, and try to be honest, loving, and full of grace — even if nobody notices.

Privately,

Dad

A VARIETY OF VERSES

You are no doubt well aware that your father is a man of many talents — runner par excellence; writer of lovely, lively prose; speaker of rare ability; guitarist of local renown. And humble, besides!

What you may not know is that I am also a poet of some distinction. Or at least I will be once the world discovers my work! And what better place and time to unveil my verse than here and now — to you, flesh of my flesh and bone of my bone.

Through the years I have penned many master-pieces, but, for brevity's sake, I offer to you only the finest. Steep your souls in the depth of these poetic truths:

The Sound of Music

I thought it must be tragic —
  The screech of tires and the roar.
I just knew that someone was injured,
  Or worse, that he was no more.

So to the place of commotion
  And chaos I swiftly ran.
I found only one deaf teenager
  With Sony Walkman in hand!

Nicknames

Some folks ooze sweet sentiment
  And play their love-word games.
We don't do much talking;
  We coin strange nicknames!

Muffin, Bean, Bub, and Blue,
  The Wagon, The Rock, The Pride.
Are these the silly words we use
  To show what love's inside?

Sweet Thing, Crit, and Yellow,
  Stace, R.J., and Sher.
Is this some cryptic dialect
  That shows how much we care?

The Children's Words

Every father dreams
  of hearing those words
that make fatherhood worthwhile:
  "Dad, you're grand!"
    "We love you, Old Man!"
      "We thank you for all you've done!"

But in the real world
　　of parents and teens
　　　there's one word he hears most of all.
Every father alive
　　can testify
　　　to the words most frequently uttered.

They're said all the time
　　with a confident grin,
　　　said over and over and over again.
"Please let me go.
　　I'll be careful, you know.
　　　And, Dad, can you spare a ten?"

Needed Reminders

Giraffes, freckles, cowlicks, and frogs;
　　Monkeys, elephants, and pug-nosed dogs;
Clover, snowflakes, and bald-headed men;
　　Gas on the stomach and the baby's grin.

Pregnant women and waddling ducks,
　　Peanut shells and the penguin's tux,
Adam's apples and missing teeth,
　　Hiccups and skinny feet.

When you pray, all somber and stern,
　　Give thanks for these and then please
　　　learn
All are here to squelch the rumor
　　That the God of life has no humor!

Ophelia Bumps

She was an old Chevy,
　　And we called her Ophelia —
　　　Ophelia Bumps, to be official,
　　Because her shocks were shot
And every ride was special.

Ophelia jarred us and bruised us
　　And jolted our necks.

She made every journey an adventure rare;
    Every passenger needed a padded posterior
And a heavy dose of devil-may-care.

But Ophelia was a lesson
    We needed to learn
        And a sermon we still need to hear:
    "On life's long road here's the operative mode —
Bumps and bruises will surely appear!"

The bard of the
breakfast table,

THE GIFT OF BEING ORDINARY

Okay, I'll admit it: I stretched the truth in the preamble to my last letter. My attempts to crow about my many talents probably fell on deaf ears anyway, so I might as well come clean: I finish with the stragglers when I race; my superb writing skill netted me exactly $17.54 on my most recent royalty check; the last sermon I delivered was noted for its mediocrity; I'm a four-chord plunker of the guitar; and, in reflecting on the poetic verse I created for you, I must admit I'm no Robert Browning. The painful, but honest truth is that I'm pretty ordinary.

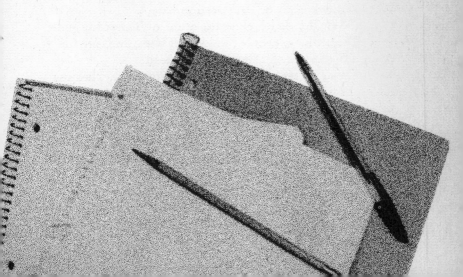

That's a tough admission to make in a competitive prove-your-worth society that worships superstars. There is a pervasive and definite idea afloat in our culture that says we're not worthy human beings unless we can hit a baseball like Dale Murphy, sing like Kenny Rogers, or act like Meryl Streep. We're definitely on the "star system" here in America, and believe that only the superbeautiful, super-talented, or superrich are successful.

I, for one, beg to differ. And I think I have the weight of Scripture on my side. When I read about the men and women God chose to do some very significant things, I realize that He has an affinity for ordinary people. Moses had a speech problem and a mean temper. Noah hit the bottle pretty heavy. Rahab was a harlot. Jonah was afraid. Hosea was a jilted husband. Ruth was from the wrong side of the tracks. Matthew and Zaccheus were hated tax-collectors. Peter, James, and John were blue-collar workers. And Paul had a pretty hefty ego.

We may look back on those people now as super-stars, but I think they were just normal folks trying to get along the best they could and to live their faith with integrity. Perhaps I'm just trying to rationalize my own "ordinari-ness," but I think God still puts His treasure in plain, clay pots (to use the apostle Paul's terminology).

Why this divine choosing of the ordinary? My guess is because ordinary people can identify with, and care for, other ordinary people. Here's what I mean.

A superstar — someone with extraordinary beauty, talent, or wealth — may become so isolated from normal folks that he or she "loses touch." The view from a pedestal is always distorted!

But when a person has both feet on the ground, has to struggle with common problems, and has to live in the real world of unremarkable kinsmen, that person can really relate. Who better to understand the woes and worries of a clay pot than another clay pot? Is this not, in fact, the whole reason behind the incarnation? The ultimate Superstar of the universe had to become "ordinary" to identify with mankind.

It is a gift to be ordinary, a gift of God that enables us to really care for other people. I don't have any trouble knowing the adolescent anguish of pimples on the face or less-than-perfect teeth, for I've been *in* that anguish. I know, too, the pain of being a second-teamer on the football squad, and what it's like to be turned down by a good-looking girl, and how it feels to drive an old jalopy to school.

Now that I'm a full-fledged "grown-up," I know about struggling for status, groping for the right vocation, juggling the bills at the end of the month, and seeing lines creep over a once-youthful face. I know about those things because I've experienced them myself as a very ordinary man.

But rather than curse God because I'm not a superstar, I've opted to look on the brighter side: How can I truly care for others if I can't identify with them? I've chosen to view my "ordinariness" as a blessing that links me to most of mankind and makes a family of us.

You two have never been ordinary to me. You have always been — and always will be — special. But just in case you never make a million bucks or star in a movie, just remember that it's a gift to be ordinary. It's okay just to be yourself, to relish living as you are, and to care for others who are ordinary too.

Ordinarily yours,

Dad

FREEDOM TO FAIL

In last Saturday's letter I told you I could identify
with those teens who are football benchwarmers, those
rebuffed by the school starlets, and those doomed to
drive beat-up cars. However, I cannot identify with those
who run for class office and get trounced. I wish I could
identify with their pain, but I can't, and the reason
is simple: I was afraid to run for office when I was in high
school (and college) because I was so fearful of failure.
It was easier to sit on the sidelines and assure myself
of universal popularity than to put my neck on the line

and risk defeat at the polls. My self-image was simply too fragile to take that chance!

When you both told me this week that you've tossed your hats into the ring for this semester's elections, I was thrilled. Thrilled because now we'll be painting placards, making up slogans, and writing campaign speeches — and all of that promises to be exciting. But thrilled even beyond that because I see that you are willing to risk; thrilled because my timidity has evidently not been passed on to you; thrilled because your egos seem to be so sturdy.

I'm currently reading a fascinating book — a magical, romantic, baseball fantasy entitled *Shoeless Joe*. I find myself underlining quite a few lines in the book — some for the poetic style of writing and some for content. One paragraph that I read and underlined just last night speaks to this issue of risking even though we might fail:

> I wish I had your passion for baseball. However misdirected it may be, it is still a passion. If I had my life to live over, I'd take more chances. I'd want more passion in my life. Less fear and more passion, more risk. Even if you fail, you've still taken a risk.[9]

That paragraph made me think not only about my high school and college fears, but also about my current fears. How long has it been since I've taken a risk? How long since I have exercised my precious, life-renewing freedom to fail?

The happiest, most fulfilling times in our lives are the times we risk: We bet our lives on a marriage partner; we gamble on a new job; we climb a mountain or run a marathon; we bring a new human being into the world; we disclose our deepest self to a trusted friend. Risk seems to be a prerequisite to adventure.

But risk and passion do not come easily to us. The rut is more comfortable. Our security is in sameness. Thoreau said, "Most men live lives of quiet desperation," but it's easier to be quietly desperate than passionately adventuresome. When we risk, we might fail or play the fool. Better safe than sorry, you know.

Or is it? Maybe that old adage has only led us to boredom. Maybe it's time to throw caution to the wind and do something risky. Maybe it's time to coin a new phrase: "Better passionate than petrified."

Obviously, I'm preaching more to myself than to you in this epistle. *I'm* the one too fragile to put my name on the ballot. You've both been bold enough to abandon safety and enter the political arena.

But I just wanted to remind *us* that we are free to risk, free to fail, free to pick ourselves up from the ashes of defeat and keep trying.

I hope you both win by a landslide. May your slogans be slick and your speeches spellbinding! But if, by some chance, you lose, remember: 'Tis better to have risked and played the fool than never to have risked at all.

Cautiously yours,

GIVE ME LIBERTY
OR GIVE ME DEATH

A churchman in a small town was famous
for using a recurring quotation in his speeches. Whether
giving a devotional in his Sunday school class or making
announcements to the congregation in a worship service,
this gentleman always worked into his spiel Patrick Henry's
famous line, "Give me liberty or give me death."

Then came a time when the local high school chapter
of the Future Farmers of America invited him to speak on
the subject "Combating Cholera in Hogs." Speculation
arose among the church members as to whether the man
would find a place for his favorite quotation in such an
address. In fact, the curiosity was so keen that a larger room
had to be found to accommodate the number of church
people who showed up.

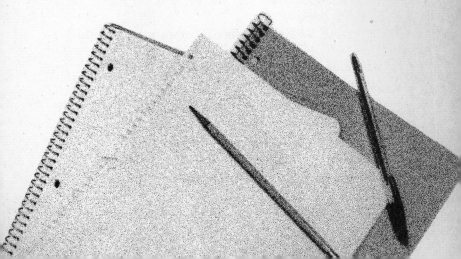

The gentleman rose to speak. "I'm very happy to be with you today. I'm also extremely excited about the topic assigned me: 'Combating Cholera in Hogs.' After all, what is cholera but a bunch of little germs running around inside a pig and screaming, 'Give me liberty or give me death!' "

I may have more in common with that speaker than I care to admit. It seems that I too have my favorite themes and, regardless of the title I put at the top of the page, I keep returning to my pet topics.

One such topic is the importance of little things, of ordinary events and common happenings. As I sort through the folders in my brain, I keep finding ones marked with this theme. When I venture to the table these Saturday mornings to put my thoughts on paper, I find that, from a number of different directions, I come at the same truth: Little things (gnats and molehills) can ruin our joy, and little things can give our lives delightful flavor.

When you were babies, I penned a song that I used to sing to you from time to time. It expressed the idea that little joys make life worth living. Picked in the key of G on the guitar, the song went like this:

It's the wonder of our babies, the sunshine in
    their eyes,
Singing "Jesus Loves Me" and countin' the stars
    in the skies;
It's readin' all those storybooks before we go
    to bed,
And knowin' that warm, warm feeling when the
    last "I Love You" is said.

It's the little things that make me happy;
It's the little things that make me smile;
It's the little things that God gives me daily
That seem to make this life of mine worthwhile.

It's the taste of rich hot cocoa on a cold and
    wintry night,
Snuggled on the sofa with the woman of my life;

It's having the joy of spending life with people
    that I love,
And knowing that those people are gifts from
    God above.

It's the little things that make me happy;
It's the little things that make me smile;
It's the little things that God gives me daily
That seem to make this life of mine worthwhile.

Those "little things" are actually not so little. In reality, they are the main ingredients in a life of joy. And there are others:

- The newspaper and a steaming cup of coffee in the morning.
- Books with shiny covers and fresh ideas.
- People who unknowingly provide encouragement because of their genuineness and faithfulness.
- The mellow, soothing sound of a Don Williams song.
- Cold days and cozy blankets.
- Swiss steak, stuffed bell peppers, homemade rolls, fruit salad, pumpkin pie.
- Enough money to pay the bills on time.
- Children with big eyes and boundless enthusiasm.
- Dreams that will one day become reality.
- Friends who listen, laugh, and encourage.

I hereby promise that this is the last list of "little things" I will give you in these letters. Forgive me if I've seemed redundant or sounded like a broken record. But if you accuse me of sounding the same theme too many times, all I can say is — "Give me liberty or give me death!"

Repeatedly yours,

Dad

LETTER JACKET DAY

I was rummaging through the closet last week and saw it hanging there. I hadn't thought about it for a long while, but seeing it in the closet flooded me with sweet memories. I was reminded of the most important day in history.

The most important day in history, just in case nobody told you, was the day the football letter jackets arrived and the coach passed them out to us. I know there have been other significant days in the annals of mankind— D-Day, Independence Day, election day, and such — but they all pale beside Letter Jacket Day.

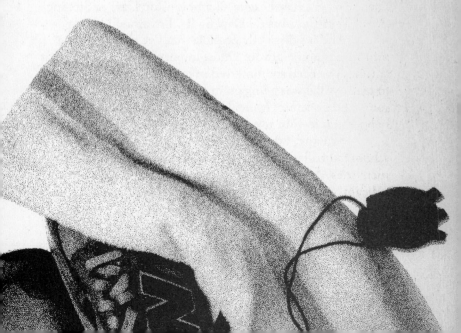

It has been over 20 years since I received the jacket, but just seeing it there in the closet gave me a thrill. The jacket still looks great — bright gold with black leather sleeves and a big, black "S" on the front. And it still fits, for I'm as scrawny now as I was then.

That jacket was more than just a jacket, of course: It was a status symbol. Of all the pieces of apparel I have ever worn, I wore that jacket with the most pride. It declared to the world my athletic prowess!

As I remember, the day after Letter Jacket Day was about 80 degrees and humid. Don't ever think, though, that it was too hot for a jacket! I wore mine, as did all the other fighting Spring Woods Tigers.

As I reflect on the glory of Letter Jacket Day, I can't help but wonder about other people's "most important days in history." Have I been insensitive to the joys that other people have experienced because their special moments seemed insignificant to me? Have I failed to see the monumental importance of Senior Ring Day, or Closing-on-the-Loan Day, or Little League Championship Day, or Singing-the-Solo-in-the-Musical Day? Sadly, I'm afraid I have.

And it's distinctly possible that I've missed the significance of some of your "most important days." I fear that at times I've been so immersed in my world that I've failed to realize what was going on in yours. If I've been callous to some of the seemingly incidental but actually monumental happenings in your lives, please forgive me.

Anyway, I think I'd better hang on to my high school football jacket. First, because it's a source of warm memories. And, second, because it reminds me that "insignificant" joys are not insignificant at all.

The Letterman,

Dad

THE PHANTOM THIEF

We have a thief at our house. He is a thief of the phantom variety, and I have never laid eyes on him. But I know he exists because some items around the house have disappeared. Not suddenly, but slowly, almost imperceptibly.

Towels, for instance. We have never, to my knowledge, thrown away a towel. Nor have we given any away. But we now have a shortage of towels around here, and I credit this shortage to the work of the mysterious phantom thief.

And he has not limited himself to towels, either. I suspect he has swiped some of my T-shirts and socks, too. If he is not responsible, where are all the T-shirts that used to fill my top drawer? And where are the matches to the lonesome socks that have somehow lost a mate? It must be the thief. He has also robbed us of combs, handkerchiefs, barrettes, stamps, and ballpoint pens. I think he has even swiped milk from our refrigerator and bread from our pantry.

The thing that makes this thief so effective is the silent, invisible way he works. He works so slowly and stealthily that his presence goes unnoticed. But towels and other items disappear nonetheless.

This same mysterious phenomenon can happen in spiritual matters, too. Slowly, bit by bit, our devotion wanes, and one day it dawns on us that we are spiritually sick. And we wonder how it happened. Reflection reveals that the thief got us.

He told us to skip worship.

He said it was legalistic to pray and read the Bible every day. He convinced us not to give our money to the hungry this month.

He assured us our one act of sin would not be noticed.

He suggested we shirk our duty just this one time.

He argued that everybody compromises somewhere along the way, so why shouldn't we?

And, unnoticeably, he robbed us of our relationship to God and left us spiritually bankrupt.

Here, then, is my warning to you: Be on the lookout for this phantom intruder. He can swipe your socks and your soul, and you'll never even know he has done his dastardly work.

The Detective,

Dad

TWO BLACK BOOKS

Have I got a deal for you! Perhaps you read about it in last Monday's *Post*. There is now a book on the market titled *IN World Guide*. It is a black-leather book with delicate, tissue-thin pages, and it details all of the "in" places in the world. All of the "in" restaurants, hotels, nightclubs, clothing stores, and not-to-be-missed places in the whole world are catalogued in the book. The cost of this indispensable guide to the good life? Only 125 dollars!

If this seems a tad high for a book, be assured that it is really a bargain. The author, a German sophisticate

named Peter Finkbeiner-Zellman, says the book should cost 500 dollars! After all, he argues, eating one disastrous meal in the wrong restaurant could easily set one back 150 dollars. You see? The book is a good investment because it prevents us from such expensive mistakes.

The author of *IN World Guide* believes the book serves three types of readers: 1) people who use it as they travel, 2) people who want to know where one should go to be "in," and 3) people who don't go anywhere but simply want to fantasize about the good life.

Interested? If so, the book is available by special order from a New York distributor.

If all of this seems ridiculous to you, it may be because you've read another black-leather Book with delicate, tissue-thin pages. This Book sells for less than 25 dollars and moves us in a different direction. It asks us, "What will it profit a man if he gains the whole world and forfeits his life?" It encourages us, "Do not lay up for yourselves treasures on earth...but lay up for yourselves treasures in heaven." It reminds us, "A man's life does not consist in the abundance of his possessions."

This second black Book calls us to scrutinize the prevalent notion that "big and expensive is always better." I, for one, am in revolt against that philosophy and hope you will join me in the revolution.

Is it always true, for example, that a 125-dollar book is more truthful than one that sells for 25 dollars?

Is it always true that caviar at one of the world's "in" restaurants is tastier than the roast beef your mother serves?

Is the agribusinessman who milks his cows with machines and tallies his profits on a computer automatically superior to the small farmer who nurtures the land his father passed down to him and who produces quality products with love?

Is the supermarket that makes great sums of money while remaining detached from its customers more successful than the family-owned grocery store built upon personal service and concern?

Is the author who writes quick, sensational thrillers that sell millions of copies a better writer than the one who makes writing a craft and who appeals to a small, discerning audience?

And is the megachurch that has grown numerically while most of its members sit on the sidelines and let the 30-member staff do the ministry really superior to the small church that is alive with love and community?

I guess I'm not very "chic" and "in," but I just can't get too excited about the *IN World Guide*. I am turned on, though, by the revolutionary teachings of that other guide for living.

Two black books. Two philosophies of life. Two tugs on the heart. And the choice is ours.

The "Out"-sider,

Dad

THE JUGGLER

Have you ever thought of the modern Christian as a juggler? Well, I hadn't either until this week, yet it strikes me as a novel but accurate way of considering our commitment to Christ. Let me try out this juggler imagery on you to see if it illumines our task as Christians.

Think of the contemporary follower of Christ as a juggler trying to handle three balls. His task is obviously tricky and demands both learned skill and a dogged determination to practice.

Label the first ball "Head," for being a Christian involves learning truth and growing intellectually. The old commandment enjoins us to love God with our minds, and

being a follower of Christ means we make a commitment to learn. The word "disciple" literally means "learner," so a vital part of the Christian life is learning to use our heads. The seasoned disciple is a seeker of truth and is always able to give a valid reason for the faith that is in him.

Did you know that many people view us who pledge allegiance to Christ as naive, deluded simpletons? And, sad to say, their estimation is often fairly accurate! Too many Christians today are ignorant of the Bible and blind to pressing social and political issues. They mouth religious cliches while playing "ostrich-in-the-sand," and there's just no depth or relevance to their faith. It is crucial for us to serve God with our minds, to explore the truth, and to be sharp, intelligent people. That's a vital, but often overlooked, part of the Christian life.

Label the second ball "Heart," for Christianity involves the heart as well as the head. Following Jesus brings a different feeling into one's life. There is more gratitude, more hope, and more jubilation. When we surrender to Him, our emotions, as well as our thought patterns, are changed. Faith involves feeling as well as fact.

Robert Frost once said that good poetry begins with a lump in the throat. I think good Christianity does, too. Through some person or event, God puts a lump in our throat, or mist in our eyes, or a song on our lips. At times we *feel* Him, and these encounters refresh us as nothing else can.

Label the third ball "Hands," for the skilled Christian juggler not only thinks and feels differently, but he *acts* differently. The Bible is full of commandments to *do* things out of love for God and people. And Jesus is explicit when He says that heaven belongs to those who *do* the will of the Father. If facts and feelings are crucial to faith, so also are fruits.

There is a lot of talk these days about "finding yourself." If you ever decide to go in search of your true identity, let me suggest a starting place: Begin with your hands, with

what you *do*. Don't listen to your voice; it will say things
that aren't really "you." Look at what your hands turn to,
and you will see who you are and what you love.

That is why Jesus was so insistent that we prove our
commitment with deeds. A commitment that just talks or
feels or thinks may be a sham. A commitment that *acts* is
inevitably genuine. Thus the indispensability of the
"Hands" ball of faith.

If we consistently drop any one of these three balls,
our Christianity is in trouble.

If we fumble the intellectual dimension, our faith
becomes a fairy tale detached from reality.

If we drop the emotional dimension, we become
stuck with dry and boring religious routine.

If we forget the works dimension, we become hypo-
crites who espouse doctrines we don't live.

But when we successfully juggle all three — Head,
Heart, and Hands — we find that our faith is a thrilling
adventure. When we mix equal doses of facts, feelings, and
fruits, our experience with Christ can sustain us through
even the worst of times.

I wish for each of you a life of joyful juggling!

Precariously yours,

THE POWER TO CREATE

In the beginning, Scripture tells us, God created man in His own image. There is no elaboration as to just what "in His own image" means, however, so we are left with the task of interpreting that phrase.

It could mean that, like God, we have the capacity to give and receive love. Or it could mean that we have a conscience, a sense of "oughtness," that is Godlike. Still another possible meaning is that God gave man freedom — freedom to choose and become what he wants to become. Certainly all three of those ideas carry some truth and may help us understand what it means to be made in God's image.

But there's another possibility, too, and it is this fourth possibility that I want to expound upon this morning. Being fashioned in God's image may mean that God

has granted us the power to create, the capacity to conceive, design, invent, and construct.

This power to create is, if you think about it, one of the trademarks of the human species. We tend to lump people into categories and classify some as creative (poets, painters, architects, etc.) and some as uncreative (secretaries, accountants, bankers, etc.). But actually all of us are, or should be, creative people. In *A Sense of the Future*, Bronowski writes, "...to my mind, it is a mistake to think of creative activity as something unusual. I hold that the creative activity is normal to all living things. Creation is the finding of order in what was disorderly, and this is a characteristically human activity."[10]

I started thinking about this remarkable gift of creativity we have been given as I was reading a book called *Religious Imagination* this week. In the book, author Robert Young says, "The world lives by the creative power in each of us. That power is the mark of God, stamped indelibly on the human race and waiting to be expressed for the good of all."[11]

I think that's true. The world lives and moves by the creative power in each of us. And our lives are enriched and made full as we use the creative power that God has implanted within us. Men, women, boys, and girls were created to create.

The child fashions his masterpiece on a piece of manila paper with stubby crayons. The sun and the grass and a square house and a bird in flight are all there. He has used his imagination and given birth to a picture. Mama, Daddy, God, and the child all celebrate his creation.

The grizzled old editor barks orders to his subordinates as he tries to get the small town weekly ready for the press. The features, the sports, the ads, and the gossip column are gathered, proofread, and carefully laid out. Wednesday night the antique press rolls. And Thursday morning the bespectacled editor drinks his coffee with paper in hand. There is a special pride in the way he inspects the headlines and reads the articles. He even turns the pages respectfully—because he's handling his own special creation.

The preacher shapes his sermon through the week and delivers it on Sunday with special pride because he and God have created a once-in-a-lifetime offering to give to the flock.

The teacher finishes her lesson plans and feels a soaring feeling inside because she and God have made a plan for learning.

The computer programmer struggles to complete his program, and when the assignment is successfully finished, he too feels a glowing sense of creation and accomplishment.

The housewife dusts and vacuums and picks up toys and cooks dinner and instinctively knows that she is creating a home and bringing something special into existence.

The writer taps a staccato rhythm on the typewriter and loses sleep to fashion her novel, but the trip to the post office to mail the manuscript makes it all worthwhile. A story has been formed out of typewritten symbols.

The father stumbles sleepy-eyed to the table on Saturday mornings and tries to make some sense of the world by scribbling a series of letters to his offspring. And there is a special satisfaction in turning a good phrase or sharing a significant truth from his experience.

The list could go on and on because the kinds of human creations are endless. All of us were made to create and, as we use our divinely given power to bring new things into existence, we will find God and ourselves and life more and more fascinating.

In the beginning, God created. Now, thanks to His love, we can too.

The Innovator,

Dad

RELIGIOUS ALLERGIES

Dennis Soyster's story is too unbelievable not to be true. I want to share it with you this morning because, if we dig deep enough, there's a moral to it that might save us from cynicism.

Dennis was told by his physician that he had an incurable disease and would not be around very long. So he panicked, stole 29,000 dollars from his employer, and proceeded to go on a merrymaking binge. He spent up to a thousand dollars an evening in one last fling before the end. Hauled into court for embezzlement, Soyster could only

plead guilty because, as his lawyer put it, he had "gone off the deep end."

This final fling might have been almost understandable, if not excusable, had not Soyster turned out to be perfectly healthy. His only problem was a lousy doctor with a faulty diagnosis. Instead of having some fatal disease, it was found that he was actually allergic to the surgical gloves used in the exploratory operation. It was the treatment itself that was causing him problems!

Before we dismiss this crazy story as a once-in-a-lifetime thing, consider how often something similar to this happens in the realm of Christian faith.

For example, someone hears a charlatan predict the end of the world on a certain day and, when it doesn't happen as prognosticated, scoffs at all talk of Christ's return.

Someone else is in a church that splits over some trivial issue and decides, after the fracas, that the universal church is demonic.

Someone else hears a radio preacher plead for money and badger his listening audience to be "generous for the work of the Lord," and decides that all Christian endeavors are a hoax.

Someone else hears a red-faced pastor scream religious cliches for an hour and concludes that the Bible has no relevance to his life.

Still another sees manipulation used in a church service and is turned off to the Good News forever.

In every one of these cases the people were simply allergic to the gloves used in the treatment of their problem. They were too blind to see that somebody's mistake in applying the gospel is not the same as the Gospel itself. Some preachers wrongly time the end of the world. Some churches squabble over incidentals. Some radio preachers prop up their egos by building a religious empire. Some pastors preach irrelevant sermons. And some churches manipulate people in the name of Jesus. But those things don't invalidate the truth of the Bible, the need for good preaching, or the importance of an "alive" church.

There is much in contemporary Christianity that needs changing, and I hope you two will not be afraid to react against what you see as obvious wrongs. Where religious bureaucracy stifles an attentiveness to individuals, stand up for love. Where a craving for institutional success overshadows obedience to God, stand up for truth. At all costs, be true to how you think God is leading you. Don't be "assembly-line" Christians with no individuality.

But be careful what you react against. Don't throw out the baby just because his bathwater is sometimes dirty. When you are tempted to "chuck" the church, or the Bible, or prayer, or any of the other "spiritual" things, remember Dennis Soyster. And don't panic or despair just because you have an allergy to the surgical gloves someone uses in trying to make you whole.

Allergically yours,

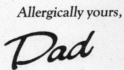

TRAVELS WITH CHARLEY

Back in the early sixties, John Steinbeck and his shaggy sidekick, a French poodle named Charley, embarked on a three-month journey throughout America. Steinbeck bought a new pickup truck, doffed its bed with a camper, installed a stove and mattress, gave his new vehicle a fancy Spanish name, and ventured forth to see America's sights and hear America's sounds. His adventures and discoveries are chronicled in the book *Travels with Charley*.

Steinbeck said that everywhere he went he met people who yearned to do what he was doing, to cut their ties and set sail on a journey, to be free to go somewhere

else and do something different, to roam and travel, to move, to be anywhere but where they were. He said this itch to take flight was prevalent in all parts of the country from Texas to Maine, Florida to Minnesota.

I suppose most of us can identify with this restlessness that makes us fidget for greater freedom and new adventures. The grass does sometimes look greener on the other side, and we long for a chance to sprawl out in it and see how it feels.

But while I recognize the prevalence of this itch to move, it worries me a bit, because I see behind it a bunch of discontented people. This popular desire to "go anywhere else" seems to portray a basic disillusionment with life the way it is. I'm afraid it shows not so much an adventuresome spirit as it does a discouraged spirit that makes one believe that anywhere has got to be better than here, that wandering around the country has got to be more fulfilling than sticking to the current routine.

In fact, I think "routine" is looked upon as one of the dirty words in our culture. The word creates images, in most minds, of drudgery, monotony, and dull repetition. Routine is what everybody in our jet-set society wants to avoid because nobody wants to move in the same rut day after day. And I guess routine has justifiably earned its reputation because it has sent many good people into boredom, depression, and breakdown. Those wanderlusters that Steinbeck met on his travels with Charley were probably sick unto sadness with routine.

But before we crucify routine as one of the terrible archenemies of mankind, let's at least give it a fair trial. Maybe, upon closer scrutiny, we will find that routine can be friend as well as foe, and we will not condemn it quite so harshly.

Routine for me, as you both well know, is coffee and the sports page every morning. Ever since I first learned to read, the awaiting sports page has motivated me to climb out of bed and face the world. Years later, hot coffee joined it as an early-morning motivator, and now I would be hard-pressed to start any day without these two companions. If the sports news gets rained on or if the coffee can in the pantry comes up empty, my whole personality changes (as, unfortunately, you also know). I become a raving madman, frantically running to the 7-Eleven store to buy my beloved *Post* or a new can of drip brew. Several times I have actually had to begin the day with one of my two friends missing, and those days have always gone miserably. On those horrible days I gained a new appreciation for much-maligned routine, and wondered how in the world I could ever criticize it.

Routine for me is also preparing and preaching sermons, reading books, listening to my favorite records, mowing grass, eating three meals a day, sleeping in that old bed we bought for nothing years ago, living and laughing with a wife and two spirited teenagers, running through our subdivision, strumming the guitar, and wrestling with what it means to be a Christian in contemporary society.

My life is really one of routine, and I know yours is too. So before we condemn routine as one of the menacing evils of the world, let's be aware that this condemnation is also a cursing of our own lifestyle.

Oh, I know that too much routine is a dangerous thing that can choke the very life out of us. I have no trouble understanding those restless people whom Steinbeck met on his journey. But I also know that routine is a wonderful thing that can lend stability, confidence, and dependability to our lives. Without routine we would become like those people in make-believe Topsy-Turvy Land who lived in a world of constant surprise and eventually lost their sanity.

There is indeed something appealing about a nomadic lifestyle that would enable us to move and escape whenever the itch strikes us: Steinbeck's camper on wheels offers a very compelling, carefree mode of living. But I suspect that even this kind of freewheeling life eventually breeds its own particular brand of disillusionment and leaves us looking for something else. Steinbeck himself was ready to go back home after his travels with Charley.

I think the path to wisdom is to try to find contentment where we are, not to chase it all over the country. So this morning I'm offering a seldom-heard cheer for routine: I propose that we recognize that routine is not always "getting in a rut," but that it can also be "finding the groove."

Routinely yours,

Dad

SOME FOUR-LETTER WORDS ABOUT SEX

Ordinarily I have two cups of coffee before writing these masterpieces. This morning I added a third cup because I need extra bolstering to address the topic I've chosen. Hopefully, a third shot of caffeine will stimulate me to venture forth some wisdom on the difficult, usually unmentionable, subject of sex.

Actually the subject is not unmentionable at all — except in the context of family life. Newspapers, magazines, television programs, and movies all blatantly parade sex before us without even a hint of embarrassment. But when I approach the subject with you, I find myself hesitant and timid. My only justification for this embarrassment is the same one I used earlier in rationalizing our unwillingness

to verbalize our love: Sacred things are cheapened by too many words. Since sex is one of the most sacred activities in human experience, I find words about it sticking in my throat.

Fortunately, it is usually easier to write words than to say them, so maybe I can write some things in this epistle that I could not say to you face-to-face. Let me give you some four-letter words about sex that I hope will clarify my feelings about it. The media and your high school crowd will certainly give you some other words about sex — words that I think don't do it justice. To balance the scale, I offer you some new words about human sexuality.

Need. Sex is one of the fundamental human needs. God has programmed sexuality into us. Some people have chosen to abstain from sexual intercourse for religious reasons or because they've opted for the single life, but that doesn't destroy their sexuality. They have just chosen not to act on those needs for some usually very good reasons.

It's important for us, though, to recognize that sexual desire and drive are part and parcel of being a normal human being. Of course we will be attracted to the opposite sex! Of course thoughts will enter our minds that we would never say out loud! Of course we will have to struggle with how to control and express our sexuality! These are issues that all humans grapple with.

We shouldn't be ashamed that we are sexual beings. To deny that we have an interest in sex is a delusion. To recognize our feelings and desires is a big step in becoming fully human.

Good. The reason some people try to hide their sexuality is that they have been taught, probably unconsciously, that sex is bad. Sadly, for many people, sex is synonymous with dirty books and pornographic movies. Naturally, they run from sex as if it were sin.

How tragic! There is not one word in Scripture implying that our sexuality is evil or displeasing to God. The *misuse* of sex is displeasing to God, but not sex itself. In fact, after God created man and woman as sexual beings, He stepped back and declared His handiwork to be delightful.

Sex is good! A sexual relationship between a husband and wife is to be a fun, liberating, ecstatic expression of commitment. If we buy into the notion that our sexuality is bad, we will deprive ourselves of some of the greatest joy that God has created for humanity.

Fear. Having chided some Christians for implying that sex is bad, let me give you this word as a corrective to the other extreme, those in our "freed-up" culture who believe that sex is good but use it wrongly.

When I use the word "fear," I'm using it in the biblical sense. When the Bible tells us to fear God, it is not so much advocating that we be afraid of Him as it is that we stand in awe of Him, respect Him, and acknowledge His holiness.

The problem with a lot of sex in our society is that there is none of this fear, or awe, in it. The impression is given that swinging and swapping and bed-hopping are a legitimate expression of our sexuality. I call it "ham sandwich sex" — go anywhere you can to get your hunger satisfied.

But the "ham sandwich" approach only leaves hungry people sad and disillusioned. A sexual relationship detached from commitment is always empty. It might provide a momentary thrill, but it won't satisfy our deep human longing to know and be known.

Only when we approach sex with awe and respect, only when we use it in the context of commitment to our marriage partner, will we find it as fun and fulfilling as it is supposed to be.

Love. This is the only word in my list you have already guessed, so I'll not belabor it. Sex *without* love is sin. Sex *with* love is heaven.

Time. Believe it or not, sex can get better as a person gets older. I suppose there comes a time late in life when the sexual thrill fades, but generally time is sex's ally, not its enemy.

When a husband and wife love each other, they grow closer as the years unfold. That closeness makes sex an even more enjoyable experience than it was when they were newlyweds.

When you get married someday, you will probably feel the same nervousness and shyness I felt when I waltzed your mother down the aisle. We had to learn together how to be sexual partners and, frankly, we were none too proficient! But time enabled us to relax, to enjoy each other, and to make sex a beautiful bond of commitment.

I tell you this because, like all the other skills in life, the expression of our sexuality must be learned and developed. And, with divine insight, God has given us the laboratory of marriage in which to hone our skills.

Gift. The best way to put it is this: Sex is a gift of God to us that is to be accepted with gratitude and treated with respect. If we fail to do either of those things, sex will not be for us what God wants it to be.

If we fail to accept sex with gratitude, it will not be as good and pleasurable as it should be. We are to be glad we have the gift!

If we fail to treat sex with respect, it will not be as sacred and meaningful as it should be. We are to treasure the gift and use it wisely!

But if we can do both of those things, we will have a priceless gift that we can open and enjoy all of our days. So be it for you two!

Thankful for sex,

Dad

SCANNING THE BOOKSHELF

I've moved my headquarters this morning from the kitchen table to my desk in the study. The reason for the switch? Well, I sat for 30 minutes in the kitchen without an ounce of inspiration, and I'm hoping that a change of scenery will get my creative juices flowing.

I'm staring now at the books on the shelves beside me, trying to think of something profound to tell you.

Maybe these books — even just the titles on them — are themselves an invitation to dialogue and a good starting place.

As I peruse the shelves, several titles strike me as provocative:

How to Talk to God When You Aren't Feeling Religious. Haven't we all been there? Don't we all wonder how we can converse with God when we feel so stale and lifeless? The key to real prayer, I think, is keeping the conversation going even when we don't feel like it.

Success Is a Moving Target. It really is. What I thought was success years ago no longer looks like success to me now. The older I get, the more success changes shape. Now, if I can be *me*, do something creative, and have a God and a few people who love me, I consider myself successful.

The Road Less Traveled. Surely that is the road we Christians should be on! We are called to be "peculiar people," set apart by different attitudes and actions. But are we? Are we really so different from the masses? Are we shaping the world, or is the world shaping us?

The Sacred Journey. Yes, I affirm that my life is a sacred journey, a pilgrimage filled with meaning and promise. All parts of it — the stumbling out of bed in the morning, the casual conversations, the daily work, the times of depression, the moments of ecstasy — are woven into a unique fabric that is special. Life *is* a sacred journey, and I must live it as such.

God Is Up to Something. I believe that, but I'm not usually expert in what that "something" is. God is so quiet and works so unnoticed that I seldom know what He is up to. But I trust that He is alive and active in my life, in our family, in our church, in our world. And I am grateful for His unseen presence.

The Reluctant Witness. We are that, aren't we? It is hard to be "salt" and "light," and most of us approach witnessing with great reluctance. Before I finish this volume of letters, I hope to include one on the difficult task of evangelism.

To Have or to Be? It seems to me that those are our two options. Either our quest is "to have," which sets us in the direction of materialism, or it is "to be," which catapults us toward quality relationships, listening to our heart of hearts, and genuinely seeking God. The title of that book spells out our options with stark simplicity.

Come to the Party. That, I think, is God's invitation to us. There's a party going on — an eternal bash of freedom and forgiveness — and we're all invited. How could anyone refuse such an invitation?

As I scan the shelves, I also see that my hodgepodge arrangement of the books has created some fascinating matchups.

For example, *Priests to Each Other* stands next to *Tomorrow's Church*, and that is an ideal partnership. In tomorrow's church, Christians are going to have to be priests to each other, to bear one another's burdens, to really care for one another, or the church will be an empty bureaucracy.

Families with Purpose stands right by *Turning to God*, and certainly any family looking for purpose can find it by turning to God in love and dedication.

When the Heart is Hungry is a neighbor to *Christ and the Meaning of Life*, reminding us that Christ is the most nourishing diet for hungry hearts.

The Silence of God is next to *Life Can Begin Again*, bearing testimony to the fact that, though God doesn't answer all our questions or solve all our problems, life can begin again if we will not give up on it.

What About Tomorrow? stands by *A Time for Boldness* on one shelf, and reminds us that we must face tomorrow's turmoil and indifference with some bold living with conviction.

Not bad arrangements, huh? I do, however, see a few books that need to be moved. *We Are Not Alone* stands much too close to *Wishful Thinking. Sermons to Intellec-tuals* is adjacent to *Ha! Ha!* and *Preaching for Today* stands by *The False Prophet.*

Those unnerve me so much, in fact, that I think I'll sign off now and find a more suitable spot for them! Until next Saturday, I am yours —

From the study,

Dad

DISCOVERING DON WILLIAMS

The purpose of this letter is two-fold: 1) to defend my taste in music and 2) to say a word about witnessing for Christ, which I promised to do last week. If I let that promise slide too long, I'll forget it for sure. First, though, I want to take up for my favorite singer and then move on to what I think is a key truth in communication.

To say that our taste in music differs is a large understatement! You like — how shall I put it? — "up-tempo" music. My taste runs to the smooth, mellow sound of country crooner Don Williams. I must admit you have been

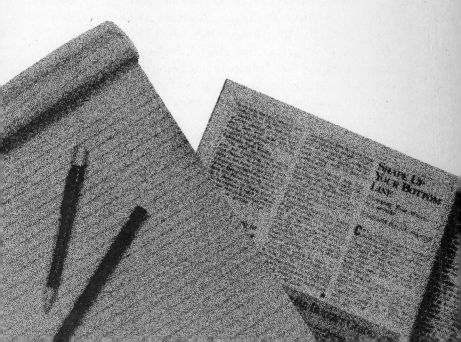

patient in letting me listen to Don, both on the car radio and the home stereo, without much complaining. But I've never been able to win you over to his country ballads. Maybe someday, when you're as old and nerve-wracked as I am, you'll appreciate Don's gentle sound.

Until just recently, I couldn't pinpoint why he appealed to me so much. His voice is rich and his songs have clean lyrics and soft, subtle harmonies, but many singers have velvet voices and sing "relaxing music." Why did I like him above all the others? The answer came after only brief reflection: I "discovered" him.

You see, 20 years ago my favorite singing group was a trio with the unlikely name of the "Pozo Seco Singers." I bought all their albums, met them briefly when they came to Baylor to sing, and spent many hours sprawled on my bed dreaming to their gentle harmony. One member of that group was Don Williams and, though the group folded in the early seventies, he persevered, put on a weather-beaten cowboy hat, and struck out on his own.

So I had actually discovered him years earlier, before anyone else knew who he was. And now when I hear him sing I go back to my younger days, when I heard his baritone in the group that sang me to sleep every night. I can still almost feel the cool breeze being cranked in the bedroom window by the attic fan and smell the roses in the Jackson's yard next door. I've known Don a long time and feel he's my private discovery.

Now for the second, "heavy" part of this letter. The point of all of this is not to convince you to listen to Don Williams. It is rather to remind you of the importance of individual discovery. We humans love to discover things.

Put a good barbecue place in the middle of busy downtown Houston and we'll drive right by it; put it way out in the country somewhere and we'll drive 50 miles to "discover" it.

Buy some clothes at Sears and you won't tell a soul about it; buy those clothes at the little shop you "discovered" in some nook or cranny somewhere and you'll tell everybody about your find.

Give me a best-selling album by a big-name artist, and I'll listen awhile and then put it away; give me one by a singer I discovered before anyone else, and I'll listen all night to its special sound.

There's just something about personal discovery that excites and thrills us.

Christian truth is most thrilling to people, too, when they discover it for themselves. Perhaps that is why Jesus told parables. That mode of communication enabled His listeners to find their own truth in the midst of a good story. Effective communication doesn't tell all the answers or solve all the mysteries. It whets the listener's appetite so he can hunt and discover for himself. And when someone finds the Good News personally, the fireworks begin!

The task of the Christian witness, then, is to whet appetites and prick interests. This is not the day of the "hard sell" in anything, especially in Christian communication. The best evangelism takes place, I think, in the context of our relationships, when we lovingly point other people to the Christ who makes such a difference. Cramming Jesus down someone's throat isn't particularly effective, but living and telling the Good News in a compassionate way can do wonders!

The question is, How do we whet appetites and prick interests? If we are to be fishers of men, how can we lure the fish? Can ordinary, timid people like us be Christian witnesses?

Well, now that I've hopefully aroused your curiosity, I think I'll deal with those questions in the next letter. Next week I'll try to make some concrete suggestions on how to help others discover Christ for themselves.

Love,

Dad

HOW TO BE A HOLE-PUNCHER

Robert Louis Stevenson once told a story that perfectly describes our calling as Christians. He said that when he was a boy he once stood on the porch of his house in Scotland watching the old lamplighter make his way down the street. As the old man lit the gas street lamps, he left flickering pools of light in the evening sky. Stevenson said he watched the scene with awe and then went running to his mother yelling, "Mother, Mother, come see a man who is punching holes in the darkness!"

That's our task as Christians — to punch holes in the darkness, to be rays of light in a world veiled with misery

and problems. The Bible says it in a variety of ways —
we are to be "salt," "light," "ambassadors," "reconcilers,"
"witnesses" — but its message is plain: The follower of
Christ is to have a positive impact on the world.

So how do we do it? As promised in last Saturday's
epistle, I want to suggest a few tangible things we can be
and do to help other people discover Christ. If we are going
to punch holes in the darkness, I think we will have to:

Be real. I mention this because I see a lot of fake
Christians these days — or at least they seem that way to
me. I don't doubt their commitment to Christ at all; I just
wish they would be ordinary human beings and not try to
be so "spiritual."

As I have told you repeatedly in these letters, it's
okay to be human, to hurt, to make mistakes, to be attracted to the opposite sex, to be your own peculiar self.
When we try to gloss our humanity with religious makeup,
we sever any chance of ordinary people identifying with us.
Ironically, our religion can be a barricade that keeps us from
knowing and loving others!

Therefore, be real! Don't be a pious actor, playing a
religious role on society's stage. Laugh. Cry. Rub shoulders
with people. Get your hands dirty. Know what's going on
in the world. And don't ever be afraid to be who you are.
After all, the word "hypocrite" literally means "one who
wears a mask," and no mask-wearer can ever be a good witness for the truth.

Be available. Someone once said that Jesus almost
never went out of His way to help anyone. After I thought
about that awhile I got the point: He was able to touch
people in the normal routine of His life. And so will we if
we make ourselves available and approachable.

Think about it: Don't you have dozens of people in
your everyday routine who are battling some kind of darkness? To be useful witnesses for Christ, you don't even have
to go out of your way! In the ordinary events of your life
you will find a mission field if you have eyes to see it.

Most of us don't have to go door-to-door passing out tracts to be "salt" and "light"; we just have to be available and sensitive in the typical daily humdrum. If we're alert, we'll spot scores of opportunities to encourage, to care, and to speak a word about Another who cares too.

Be accepting. The Christian persuader is not a religious answer-person with a machine-gun approach to communication: Line 'em up and mow 'em down with theological propositions. The effective witness is a person who listens and takes the time to know other people. If we take the approach that we've got it all together and we're going to straighten out a bunch of pagans, we'll fall flat every time. No one likes to be looked down upon or treated as a "prospect."

Our goal is to enter into dialogue, to hear another person's story, and then to tell our own. We usually have to earn the right to engage in such a dialogue, for few people can speak of sacred things with a stranger. But if we can learn to accept people where they are and love them where they are, we've taken the crucial first step in communicating the Good News of Christ.

Here's an idea I heard that helps me be more accepting, especially when I'm trying to relate to a person who is basically "unlovable." Someone has said, "See a man as he is, and he will stay as he is. See a man for what he can become, and someday he will become it." When we can see a person for what he or she can become, we're on the road to acceptance and good communication.

Be captivated. Perhaps I should have put this at the top of the list. If we're not captivated by Christ and thrilled with what He is doing in us, we're not going to be very effective witnesses. Even if we are real, available, and accepting, the salt will have no savor if we're not personally enthused about our journey with Christ.

Certainly we'll not always be "on fire." The "3-D's" of the Christian life—Doubt, Depression, and Drudgery—will occasionally pour cold water on the flames of our fervor. I've already claimed my place as president of The Roller Coaster Club, so you know I'm no expert at staying on spiritual mountaintops.

But even in our "down times," we can know that spiritual truths are the bedrock of our life. We can hang in there because we're still loved by God. Remember, we love Him because He *first* loved us.

When I speak of being captivated by Christ, I'm talking about giving a resounding *yes* to these kinds of questions: Is my relationship to Christ important to me? Do I have anything I'd like other people to find? Does my faith give my life purpose? Am I growing and becoming? Do I have hope on even the darkest nights?

If we can say yes to those questions, we're on the way to helping others find Christ. For sharing the Good News is not a packaged program or the memorization of a plan; it is a way of life that declares that Christ really makes a difference. If we have that, we have more than any canned approach to evangelism will ever give us.

To put it simply, when it comes to witnessing we're not pushy salesmen but satisfied customers! We've tried the product and found it revolutionary!

These four ideas — be real, available, accepting, and captivated — seem to me to be indispensable spokes in the wheel of evangelism. I know there are other plans and programs, but many of them don't fit my personality and probably don't fit yours either. By all means feel free to experiment and find your own way of conveying the Good News.

But always remember this: There is no greater joy in life than lighting a little flame in a dark, dark sky.

Yours for a life
of punching holes,

OLD SLOWPOKE

I nearly ran over a turtle yesterday. He was making his way across the busy road at a normal turtle's pace, and I had to swerve to avoid crushing him. I couldn't help but wonder what Old Slowpoke was thinking as the cars whizzed by and over him. Surely he must have felt terrified, confused, and helpless as he inched his way across the pavement. One thing I know: Old Slowpoke quickly assumed a defensive posture after the shadow of my car passed over him. As I glanced back at him in my

rearview mirror, I saw him pull his head quickly into his shell and wait for the inevitable to happen.

Old Slowpoke may well be the most accurate symbol for today's average American. It seems to me that more and more people are feeling like that hard-shelled turtle on the busy road — terrified, confused, and helpless to do anything about their situation. Ours is now a society of locked doors and burglar alarms. Our neighborhood signs no longer welcome visitors but, instead, warn intruders of our patrol program. Strangers are viewed with suspicion, and cohorts are seen not as comrades, but as competitors. We have learned some painful, painful lessons: Most people can't be trusted; life is complicated; answers don't come cheap; and nobody escapes the human condition unscathed.

With these beliefs in mind, the normal human responds just like Slowpoke. He pulls back in his shell and tries to hide, all the while waiting for catastrophe to hit. Like my turtle friend, people are assuming a defensive posture toward others. They are afraid to venture out into new relationships or deepen existing ones because they don't want to run the risk of being hurt, rejected, or abused. The safest response to the perils around us seems to be to curl up in a brick house and hope the world won't crush us.

But anyone who claims to follow Christ has to refuse this turtle philosophy. Our symbol is a cross, which reminds us that our way is one of risk, love, and even pain. The Christian is the one person with the courage to get involved with people. The Christian is the one person gullible enough to trust both God and His creatures. The Christian is the one person foolish enough to believe that all things are working together for his good. And the Christian is the one person loving enough and genuine enough to coax a few other people out of *their* fearful shells.

It dawned upon me, as I was contemplating the last couple of letters I'd written you, that the whole biblical idea of witnessing and influence is a rejection of the turtle philosophy. In other words, all I wrote you in the previous two epistles is predicated upon our willingness to take off the shell and run some relational risks.

If our basic philosophy of life is to "look out for number one," we'll never even care about being "salt" and "light." When we become *self*-centered and *self*-oriented, we might feel safer, but we'll never be particularly happy. Human beings just don't thrive in shells — even relational ones they fashion themselves. We're made to give and receive love!

With abandon,

Dad

CAUGHT IN THE MIDDLE OF OURSELVES

Confession Time: Everything I've written in the last few letters is true. Everything I've written in the last few letters goes against my basic temperament.

To put it starkly, I *write* about witnessing for Christ much more easily than I *do* it. I can easily tell you not to live by the turtle philosophy, but I have a natural tendency to be like Old Slowpoke myself. In short, I'm feeling guilty about writing things I have so much trouble living.

Dr. George Sheehan once wrote:

When I was young, I knew who I was and tried
to become someone else. I was born a loner. I came into
this world with an instinct for privacy, a desire for solitude, and an aversion to loud voices, to slamming doors
and to my fellow man. I was born with the dread that
someone would punch me in the nose or, even worse,
put his arm around me.

But I refused to be that person. I wanted to be-
long. Wanted to become part of the herd, any herd.
When you are shy and tense and self-conscious, when
you are thin and scrawny and have an overbite and a nose
that takes up one third of your body surface, you want
friends, you want to join with others. My problem was
not individuality, but identity. I was more of an individual than I could handle. I had to identify with a
group.[12]

I may not be quite as introverted as young Dr.
Sheehan, but I'm in the same ballpark somewhere. It is not
my natural bent to be chummy, open, and outgoing. I have
had to struggle with those biblical passages about going public with my faith, and I suspect you will too. Both of you
are more gregarious than I am, but I still see much of myself
in you — a need for privacy, a desire to leave people alone,
a dislike of backslapping and joke-telling. Sad to say, both
of you are fashioned a bit in your father's image.

What I have said about influencing other people for
Christ does not mean we have to have a personality trans-
plant and radically change who we are. What I hope you
will be able to do is find your own style of being "salt" and
"light," to use your natural temperament to punch some
holes in the darkness. When we try to be someone we're
not, we actually sabotage any hope of pointing others to
Christ. As I underscored a couple of weeks ago, we have to
be real to be effective communicators.

One of the most miserable times of my life was my
freshman year in college, simply because I tried to be

someone I wasn't. I decided to be Mr. Big on campus, and so I affected an air of confident congeniality. I joined clubs, went to parties, shook hands, slapped backs, and tried desperately to be impressive. One of my biggest fears was that I would come to the end of my college career and have no distinctions or achievements beside my name in the school yearbook! So I worked hard at being "important."

You know what I learned? Facades are too heavy to wear for very long! I quickly grew weary of being a fraud, and decided to just be myself. And I started enjoying school and life a whole lot more as the real me. I was able to find a few close friends and a few extracurricular activities, and I had a fine time the rest of my college days.

My problem was trying to be the proverbial square peg in the collegiate round hole. When I admitted I was a square, I found some square niches to fit in, and life became much more enjoyable.

This is one of the tensions we will have to face all our days: How can we be private people and public witnesses? How can we be square pegs when the Bible seems to call us at times to fill round holes? I wish I could tick off four quick points and a jazzy poem to resolve that tension, but I can't. I wish you well as you wrestle with it.

Of course this witnessing issue is just one of many issues that relate to a broader tension — the tension between who we are and who we think we ought to be. In case you hadn't noticed, this tug-of-war between our "ideal self" and our "real self" is one of the real dilemmas of being human. Let me introduce the opposing forces in this tussle.

Pulling on one side of the rope is our "ideal self," or the person we think we ought to be. Obviously, all of us can use some improvement. To shrug our shoulders and say we can't change or that we're just not the type to do something is a denial of our God-given power to grow. Our "ideal self" is a needed target that pulls us toward perfection. This image of the person we ought to be pulls at us constantly, and it has plenty of muscle!

On the other end of the rope is our "real self," or the person we are. Our "real self" includes our flaws as well as our strengths. It constantly feels pressure from the "ideal self" and, if pulled too long and hard, will grow discouraged and give up. Because it cannot measure up to the perfection which the "ideal self" demands, the "real self" can just sit down and decide it's not worth the fight.

Now let me be more concrete and give you some specific examples of this tug-of-war in our lives.

The "ideal self" tells us to witness with boldness; the "real self" tells us to stay to ourselves.

The "ideal self" tells us to study for the exam; the "real self" wants to go to bed early.

The "ideal self" encourages us to be the life of every party; the "real self" wants to find a good friend and converse in the corner.

The "ideal self" tells us to go out for athletics; the "real self" knows it would be better off in the band.

The "ideal self" suggests that we dress up to go to the mall; the "real self" would be more comfortable in shorts and a T-shirt.

Add to the list as you like, but I think you get my point. The struggle between who we think we ought to be and who we really are is inescapable. If you feel that tug-of-war at times, welcome to the human race!

As I said, there's no easy solution to this dilemma, but I will offer you this one piece of wisdom: Don't neglect either of your "selves." Try to keep them in comfortable tension.

If you neglect your "ideal self," you'll grow slack about witnessing, studying, or any other disciplines that don't come easy for you. That picture we have in our heads of who we ought to be is a gift that helps us become more than we are. Certainly, the picture of our "ideal self" can become distorted and inaccurate, but generally it is a needed challenge to keep us "becoming."

If you neglect your "real self," you'll never have a unique identity or be able to enjoy being you. You see, contrary to the fierce tugs of ideal, you really don't have to be the life of every party, the star of the basketball team, or a straight-A student. You can just be you.

I wish I could bring you a report from "over the hill" that this tug-of-war is only a teenage phenomenon. If anything, though, the tugs have intensified for me through the years, and I'm still caught squarely in the middle of them.

But the middle, I've learned, is not a bad place to be. It enables us to feel the challenging tug of self-expansion and the comforting tug of self-acceptance. If we can learn to balance the tensions on each side, we can feel good about our "real self" and still try to become the valid parts of our "ideal self."

Well, I need to sign off and hit the road. I want to get in my morning run before it gets too hot, and it's already 7:30.

Sorry I can't ease the tensions of being human for you. Just know, when the tugs come, that you're not the only ones feeling them.

In the middle too,

ANALYZING ANALYZING

I wandered by the television Thursday morning and flipped on The Donahue Show. The topic of discussion was human sexuality, and I decided to watch awhile.

The expert on the subject was a portly, middle-aged woman and, from what I heard, she knew her subject well. She told me and all the others in television land what intimacy means to a man and what intimacy means to a woman. She told us exactly how the males and females differ emotionally and what a man wants from a woman and vice versa. She spoke with unquestionable authority, but after about ten minutes I switched her off and went on my way.

The discussion had become so analytical and scientific that intimacy sounded very drab and uninviting. Talking about intimacy, I realized, is just not the same as being intimate. One is cold, clever dissection; the other is warm, passionate feeling. And it seemed to cheapen intimacy to talk about it like it was a laboratory rat.

Our scientific age, though, has made analyzers of us all. (Note my last letter analyzing our two selves.) We are trained from the crib to observe, formulate, hypothesize, and compartmentalize. A little analysis is wonderful for comprehending our world, but too much mental rumination can destroy our spontaneity. We can become so engrossed in trying to understand life that we fail to enjoy it! Most things are better experienced than analyzed.

I know, for instance, that experiencing a flower is much more fun than hearing a botanist's explanation, brilliant though it might be, of how chlorophyll works. The flower loses something in the translation.

I know, too, that experiencing a person is a lot more entertaining than trying to psychoanalyze his personality. A little bit of personality dissection might be good and helpful, but too much of it destroys the genuineness of the person before us. People, like flowers, are to be experienced, not analyzed. The same is true for sunsets, ice cream cones, kisses, and most of the other really important things in life.

And it's true, too, of our Christianity. The Christian way loses something when it becomes a cold research topic. The preacher can know every verse in Scripture that has the word "grace" in it, but he doesn't really know a thing about grace until he feels it in his bones and dances through life because of it. The Bible teacher can list the ten steps to happiness as found in the Sermon on the Mount, but she doesn't really know a thing about her subject until she sings in the shower. A man can know Greek and Hebrew and call himself a scholar, but he doesn't know the Bible at all until he has been brought to his knees by its overwhelming message.

There is a marked difference, you see, between knowing the Good News and feeling it. The Christian gospel, like all the other sacred things of life, is much better experienced than analyzed.

So I'm glad I flipped on the tube Thursday. That brief exposure to the sex expert reminded me of something I need to tell you: Intellectual people analyze life; happy people live it.

Happily,

Dad

LIVING WITH STYLE

What you do with the future is, of course, your own business. We will be standing on the sidelines rooting you on and offering advice, if asked for, but the days of our "pulling your strings" are about over.

Gradually you have assumed control of your lives, and that's the way it should be. Maturity is the process of accepting responsibility for your own destiny, and wise parents understand that children are born to be eventually set free, to follow their own head, and to find their own way.

That's not to say that all parents can comfortably allow their offspring that freedom. Frankly, when one has

spent years trying to get a kid to brush her teeth, pick up her clothes, do her homework, and a multitude of other duties, it's not easy to let go and trust that child to make it on her own. If we occasionally lapse into barking orders and nosing into your business, just chalk it up to parental conditioning.

But you are both perched at the door of high school graduation, and my objective mind tells me to let you go, to grant you liberty, to allow you to test your wings. I'll try to heed that objective mind as much as I can, but I make no grandiose promises. These letters themselves are evidence that I tend to be the local dispenser of wisdom and insight. When I push too hard or speak too much, please forgive me and remember everything I've ever written or told you about grace.

Whatever you choose to do with your lives, I hope you'll do it with style. By "style" I'm referring to a sense of craftsmanship, of performing your duties with an artistic flair that shows you care for what you're doing. Remember that word "acedia" I used when writing about the man with the steam engine? Acedia, which means sloth or care-lessness, is the opposite of living with style. It is a slaphappy, bland way of going about life that is the antithesis to the craftsman's touch.

Life is supposed to be the offering up of ourselves to God. We are to offer Him something that nobody else in the whole universe can give Him — our own particular gifts. We are to offer Him our "peculiar treasures" — the ability to paint or cook stew or type letters, the gift of listening or supervising or writing.

The poet Gerard Manley Hopkins once wrote:

Each mortal thing does one thing and the same:
Namely, to be itself and nothing more,
Crying, "What I do is me; for that I came."

Doing with love and style that for which we came is the highest gift we can give to God.

I guess what I'm trying to say is that we are to be artists in what we do, artists in the sense that Kenneth Clark was talking about when he said, "Everything done for the glory of God should be the finest and most splendid which the mind of man could devise or his hand execute."[13] In the broadest sense of the word, an artist is one who does something with dignity, grace, and order. The work of our hands, then, ought to be art for God.

Of course, this living with style I'm attempting to portray doesn't apply just to the days ahead or to a future job. This very day each one of us will make our personal offering at the altar of the Most High. How we treat the customers, write the article, teach the class, take care of the house, program the computer, bake the bread, or sing the song is our gift to God today.

The French novelist Francois Mauriac once commented, "My writings have benefited from the fact that, no matter how lazy I was, I always wrote the least article with care, putting my whole soul into it."[14] When we can do the least thing with care and put our whole soul into it, we have learned the meaning of Christian discipleship.

Let us always do the work of our hands with dignity and joy so that we can avoid shoddy discipleship and careless living. I'm convinced that the people who make life worth living — whatever their education, vocation, or financial status — are the people who do even the little things with care, who see every situation as an opportunity to make an offering to God.

That is the challenge I place before you this Saturday morning. Run from slipshod workmanship. Flee sloth. And, whether playing the guitar or planting a garden, be an artist for God.

Carefully,

Dad

TRUTH GRAB-BAG

When I embarked on this mission of correspondence ten months ago, one fear haunted me — that I would run out of "soap" after only a few letters. I didn't enter this project with a set outline of topics to address, though I did have a vague notion as to some of the themes I thought were important. I decided, rather, to take the "hang loose" approach and respond to life as it unfolded. I had no guarantee that ideas would come, and I was afraid my wisdom would run out before my allotted year was up.

Well, my fears were in vain. Topics have come like manna in the wilderness, and every Saturday I've had something to write. Some of it may not have been earth-shattering

in its profundity perhaps, but at least I've never left you a blank letter! There have been a few weeks when the manna came just in the nick of time, but it has always come and I've always enjoyed serving it to you. I hope you've found a few tasty morsels along the way.

My problem now is not too "little" to say but too *much*. In a few weeks our year is up, and I realize I've got more to tell you than I have Saturdays on which to write. We could go another year, I suppose, but I still have the fear that the manna supply will cease. Besides, I don't want to press my luck. You've indulged the Old Man for almost a solid year, and I don't want to impose upon your kindness any longer. A promise is a promise — I'll wrap up my coffeepot correspondence in seven weeks.

But just to make sure I touch or retouch all the philosophical and theological bases, I want to offer you a potpourri this week. I offer you a grab-bag of assorted tidbits, recognizing that each tidbit could be the subject of a whole letter (or even a whole book!). Take what nuggets you find especially truthful; discard the others in your brain's garbage disposal.

Here we go:

- We always make time for those activities we consider vital to our lives. "I just don't have time" is not as honest as "I'm just not interested."
- The worst enemy of comfortable America is boredom. Though we spend millions of dollars on pleasure and entertainment, our boredom lingers.
- Money has little to do with joy because it cannot purchase creativity, companionship, or commitment.
- Society cannot define success. Each individual must decide for himself the meaning of the word.
- The people we love most are the people at whom we get the angriest. Love and anger seem to use the same doorway.
- Video games do frightening things to a person's blood pressure.

- The world is not miserable for lack of justice; its misery stems from an absence of grace.
- We are all blind to our worst faults.
- Both happiness and unhappiness are uncontrollably contagious.
- Laughter really is the world's best medicine.
- Hope usually arrives in small packages — a phone call, a glance of approval, a child's laughter, a gust of wind on your face.
- Every person must find his place. The marathoner and the middle linebacker can't play the same game well.
- Life void of God is a wasteland.
- The person to be pitied most is the one who can no longer cry.
- Every person you will meet today is waging some kind of personal battle.

Brimming over,

Dad

I NEVER SAID I WAS A VETERINARIAN

I have now officially verified it: Pride *does* go before a fall. Last Saturday I donned my professor's cap and glibly tossed you some precious gems of truth. I felt pretty comfortable in the wise man's role and was starting to envision myself as quite an expert on life. I saw myself finishing off these letters with a flourish of deep truths that would leave you marveling at my insight.

Father, the Infallible Informant of All of Life's Mysteries. Father, the Inerrant Guide to the Good Life.

Then yesterday afternoon Critter had her kittens, and my whole charade went up in smoke. You were kind not to say "I told you so," but I saw it in your eyes. You had both tried to convince me that Critter was great with kitten, but I only laughed at such a foolish suggestion.

How could a cat as young and tiny as Critter give birth? Sure she had gotten a little bloated around the middle lately, but hadn't the vet told us just a few months ago that she just naturally looked swollen? Hadn't he said himself that she wasn't even a year old and not yet a serious candidate for motherhood?

So when we discovered those four scrawny creatures on the old bed in the garage, I was shocked. Critter never got *that* big, at least not big enough to carry four babies. But the births happened and, as if to remind me of my error, she took each kitten by the scruff of the neck and marched all four into *my* room and deposited them under *my* dresser! Their squeaks in the night are irritating reminders of my fallibility.

What did I learn from this experience? Well, several things:

- Young, small cats *can* have kittens.
- Cats don't have to look very pregnant to have kittens.
- Even though I've unloaded a ton of wise words on you, I'm not infallible and had better not be too dogmatic.
- One's children, on rare occasions, can be right and should be listened to.
- It is possible to have a long list of reasons for your opinion and still be dead wrong.
- When wrong, it is best just to admit it and dine on humble pie.
- Grace really is amazing.

The first six on that list follow logically from the birth incident; the last item may not seem to follow so naturally. How did I get from Critter's kittens to the grace of God?

Easy! Any time we face up to our fallibility, our sin, our wrongheadedness, we have to head in one of two directions: We either get angry at our error-proneness and head toward despair, or else we acknowledge our limitations and head toward grace. Need I tell you which is the better option?

We have sung it hundreds of times — "Amazing Grace." But only when we face up to who we actually are do we realize just how amazing grace really is.

We make loud pronouncements about cats and other things that are completely off-base, but God laughs at our foolishness and still accepts us.

We try our best to interpret Scripture, learn doctrine, hear the voice of God, and live righteously, yet we never get it all together; but God still loves us and calls us His own.

We stumble into sin with daily regularity, but God still sees us as perfect as we ask to be forgiven.

We get discouraged and dejected, but God comes in some small, unnoticed way to buoy our steps and pat us on the back.

We struggle and strain to be good, to be right, to be impressive, but God tells us to relax, that He's taken the pressure off by sending His Son to die on the cross.

The biblical word for all of these realities — God's acceptance, no-strings-attached love, forgiveness, encouragement, and freedom — is grace. And grace is amazing! It's the key ingredient in a life of joy. Without it even the Christian life becomes a heavy burden and a weary keeping of commandments. But with it life overflows with gladness. The Christian life *without* grace is a life of obligation. The Christian life *with* grace is a life of celebration.

Hooray for Critter and her kittens! Hooray for my false diagnosis and another reminder of my fallibility! Hooray for another occasion to thank God for His amazing grace!

Before you toss all these letters in the trashcan because I've shown my true blundering colors, remember this: I never once claimed to have a degree in veterinary medicine.

The mistaken one,

Dad

SINGING IN THE SNOW

Let me give you a flesh-and-blood example of what an absence of grace can do in our lives. The woman I'm about to describe is nobody in particular, but I'd wager you know her or someone like her.

She is a fine woman. Ask all who know her, and they will readily agree. Her morality and character are above reproach. She teaches a Sunday school class and is at church every time the doors open. Her knowledge of the Bible is impressive, and she is often held up as the model Christian.

But something is wrong. She is rigid and dogmatic about her convictions. Those who know her best

testify that she seldom smiles. And they've never heard her really laugh. The joy that is supposed to be her Christian birthright seems to be absent. She is righteous but joyless, faithful but tired. Though she is not even aware of it, she is a victim of graceless piety.

Recognize her? I imagine you do, because her brand of religion is very much in evidence these days. Religion, you see, is a taxing thing. It demands more of us than we can ever produce. Try as we might to be and do right, we can never be and do enough. Even our finest, most zealous righteousness turns out to be filthy rags. In frustration, we either despair and quit or smile bravely through our misery. We come out either washed up or run down.

Because religion is so exacting, it comes as awfully Good News to read the New Testament and to discover that Christianity is not a religion at all. Robert Capon, in his book *The Youngest Day*, says it eloquently:

In the long run, Christianity is not a religion. While it uses the forms of religion—while it has observances, days and seasons that seem to be intended to fix up our relationship with God and the universe — it is in fact the announcement of the end of any need for such influencing at all. It is the proclamation of the gospel that God has fixed up everything himself and it is an invitation to believe that incredibly cheerful piece of good news.[15]

Here's the difference in a nutshell: Religion asks more than we can ever deliver. The gospel gives more than we can ever repay. What a difference! The key ingredient in that difference is the grace I wrote about last week. Grace is the difference between working to earn God's love and rejoicing because we already have it. Get a good dose of God's grace in your veins, and you'll never lack for joy!

If I had to wish just one thing for you two, I would wish that you find joy in your relationship to Christ. I see so many people (not just old people, I might add) like the woman I just described to you: serious, pious, honest—

but sorely lacking in joy! Get a church full of those people together and you'll have a funeral, not a festival of Good News.

There's an old story about Francis of Assisi that I'd like to believe is true. It seems a band of robbers fell upon him as he journeyed through the woods and robbed him of his meager possessions. Imagine their surprise when they released him and heard him go singing his way through the snow!

What those robbers didn't know was that Francis' real treasure was untouchable. They could take his coat and coins, but his trust in God and his experience of grace were eternally locked in his heart. When you have that kind of treasure, you can sing even in the snow.

I wish for you that treasure, but I cannot give it to you. It must come from Someone Else. But if you know of grace, and the joy that always travels with it, you will never be poor.

Singing this Saturday,

MY FANTASY

I've been poking around the subject of joy in the last couple of letters, so I think I'll tell you one of my fantasies. When pressure builds or life gets drab, I flip on this fantasy in my mind and escape reality for awhile. Just thinking this dream nudges me toward joy.

In my fantasy world, I live in the country in a log cabin. My cabin has a covered back porch, and on that porch I sip coffee each morning while watching my Hereford cows grazing down by the pond. Then I saunter over to my rolltop desk and give attention to my vocational pursuit — the writing of books, each of which is eagerly awaited by millions of readers. After writing flowing prose

for a few hours, I eat lunch, take a nap, and then resume writing until dinner. After dinner I stroll the cool countryside with your mother. We count stars as they appear, enumerate our blessings, and rejoice in the goodness of God. Home again, we read awhile and then crawl into bed relaxed and content.

How does that grab you? Just writing that fantasy makes me feel warm all over! Even if that dream never comes true, it serves me well. I always have a place to run to when the real world gets too heavy.

You know what I notice about my fanciful vision? It is free of pressure and hassle. In my log cabin I don't have to deal with cantankerous people, traffic jams, noise pollution, job deadlines, and all the other stresses I have in my real life. One reason this fantasy appeals to me, I think, is that it removes me from stress. Log cabins and best-sellers are attractive, but the real intrigue of my imagined life of seclusion is its relaxed pace. In my dream world all is joy and laughter, with never a churning stomach or tension headache.

Sounds great, doesn't it? Don't you ever dream of a world free of schoolwork, grade pressures, peer expectations, and an uncertain future? Don't you ever wish you could hop on a sailboat and head to faraway islands of adventure?

We are certainly not the first people harboring secret thoughts of escape. Even the prophet Jeremiah, several thousand years ago, dreamed of finding a little roadside motel where he could prop up his feet and take it easy for a spell. He too wanted to get away from conflict and hassle and to shed the shackles of real life in ancient Judah.

Pressure-free living is alluring, but — and I hate to be the one to break the news to you — impossible. Waiting for a world in which there is no stress means waiting for a world we will never have. As long as we're alive and kicking, we'll have some hassle.

That's the bad news. The good news is that stress, when applied in moderate doses, actually works *for* us. It prods us to change and grow. It keeps us alert and on our toes. It pushes us to do new things and to look for creative solutions.

Dr. George Sheehan reminds all of us escapist, log cabin types:

There is a tendency these days to see mental pressure as something to be avoided. We view mental health as a state in which we are free from the feeling that there is something wrong with us; free from the need to become more and more; free from the tension between what we are and what we should be.

Actually, it is quite the opposite. Mental health comes with the ability to live with these feelings, these needs, these tensions. These pressures are as essential as they are unavoidable.[16]

Pressure *is* unavoidable. But as long as it is not too oppressive, it can help us grow as human beings.

Don't feel bad if you have a fantasy world that is free of strain and struggle. You *need* a good imagination to cope with the gnats and molehills of reality! But just remember that our fantasy worlds are just that — fantasies. Anyway, with my luck, my back porch would get termites, my cows would contract some awful disease, and my books would be monumental flops. *Then* I'd find out the real meaning of pressure!

Hangin' in there,

Dad

CHET ATKINS AND JESUS

Supposedly this is a true story. I heard it on the radio from comedian Jerry Clower, so you might want to take it with a grain of salt. But he said the story is true.

Chet Atkins, the great guitarist, got to feeling tired and burned out several years ago. He was fed up with the pressures and hassles of the music business, so he decided to escape. He boarded an ocean freighter, grew a beard, and for a solid month served as a deck hand at sea.

One night the boys on board broke out a guitar and had a songfest. The guitar was passed around the circle, and

everybody got a turn to play. Eventually the guitar came to Chet Atkins. He played a few tunes and then handed the instrument to another sailor.

After the guitar had made the rounds, someone began to rant and rave about the way that one guy played. Mighty impressive, the others agreed.

The freighter captain was not so easily impressed, however. "Not bad," he admitted, "but he ain't no Chet Atkins."

I chuckled when I heard that tale, but then sobered when I realized that another celebrity often goes unnoticed in a crowd. Scripture says that an incognito Guest escapes our attention most of the time:

They also will answer, "Lord, when did we see thee hungry or thirsty or a stranger or naked or sick or in prison, and did not minister to thee?" Then he will answer them, "Truly, I say to you, as you did it not to one of the least of these, you did it not to me" (Matthew 25:44,45).

According to these verses, Jesus assumes the disguise of "the least of these," and many of us don't even recognize Him.

Have you ever considered the fact that old Mrs. Lucas in the dilapidated house down the street is Jesus in disguise? That in failing to visit her, call her, or take her fresh vegetables we are neglecting Christ Himself?

Is it possible that the overweight, homely girl huddled alone in the corner of the school cafeteria is actually the Son of God looking for a friend?

Can it be that those hollow-eyed, malnourished children on the six o'clock news stare at us through divine eyes? That in withholding food from them we are starving our Lord?

Sadly, tragically, I'm afraid that it's so. Christ tells us to look for Him in the unlikely garb of "one of the least of these," and anytime we neglect the usually-neglected we turn our backs on Him.

How then do we learn to recognize Christ in our world? I think we can start by remembering the slogan that was once posted at every railroad crossing: "Stop, Look, and Listen." That simple formula will go a long way in making us more sensitive.

· *Stop*. *Stop* treating people the way everyone else does. *Stop* being totally preoccupied with ourselves. *Stop* thinking that real living is acquiring a bunch of expensive trinkets. *Stop* running around in a flurry of mad activity. *Stop* seeing people as "just people" and begin seeing them as Christ in disguise.

· *Look*. *Look* at individuals, not groups. *Look* at old Mrs. Lucas, the girl in the cafeteria, the gaunt child on television. *Look* beneath the surface to see the hopes and hurt in people's eyes. *Look* beyond our pleasure to see another person's necessity.

· *Listen*. *Listen* to the pain of the world, as unpleasant as it is. *Listen* to individual stories — the death of Mr. Lucas, the cross-country move that put the girl in that lonely corner of the cafeteria, the wail of the baby with no milk. *Listen* not just to our needs but to the needs of the human family as well. And *listen* to a still, small voice within us to hear what we should do to make a difference.

That may not sound very profound, but it's a starting place. If some sophisticate says that our "Stop, Look, and Listen" philosophy is too shallow and naive, we can just point to Jesus Himself who truly lived by that slogan. He always seemed to *stop* amid frenzy, *look* at specific people, and *listen* to them long enough to change their lives. If "Stop, Look, and Listen" was good enough for Jesus, it's good enough for me.

Even as I write this to you I'm made aware again that I write a whole lot better than I live. I'm sure I've been insensitive to you many times, so there's no telling how often I've stumbled blindly by the needs of strangers. But I'm working on it. And I pray frequently that Christ will do for me what He did for that man in Mark's Gospel — give me a "second touch": "Then again he laid his hands upon his eyes; and he looked intently and was restored, and saw everything clearly" (Mark 8:25).

Jerry Clower's story about sailors not recognizing Chet Atkins is worth a few chuckles. Jesus' story about good people not recognizing Him is worth a few tears.

Makes you pause for reflection, doesn't it?

In process,

Dad

SURE COULD USE
A LITTLE GOOD NEWS

The news in this morning's *Post* was even drearier than usual — a case of serious child abuse in Houston, another plane taken hostage, more ominous rumblings between the U.S. and the U.S.S.R., economic indicators on the downswing, etc. I find myself humming Anne Murray's song of a few years back: "Sure could use a little good news today."

Which leads me to my theme of the morning — the Good News that is the heart of Christianity. If we know this Good News, we can read that awful stuff in the morning paper and still face the day with confidence.

If I had to put the essence of the Good News in a few sentences, here's the way I'd do it: "The Good News of Christianity is that God loves us. The One who sprinkled the stars into space takes delight in us as individuals. He wants us to be happy. He wants us to love and be loved. He wants us to find our place in the world and make our special contribution. In short, God is *for* us."

It's amazing how we Christians forget this Good News and instead live and teach something that sounds like bad news. The best news ever sounded on planet Earth somehow comes out as dry, dusty doctrine that no one wants to touch with a ten-foot pole. I'm afraid that the modern church has so garbled the Good News that most people now think of Christianity as the boring memorization of a set of religious rules. How sad! We have succeeded in making the Christian life a somber march rather than a joyful dance.

Our forefather, Jonathan Edwards, once preached a famous sermon called "Sinners in the Hands of an Angry God." He pictured God dangling people over the flames of hell, ready to drop them into eternal torment. Though he reportedly read the sermon in a monotone voice from a written manuscript, the congregation fell into weeping and fits of emotion.

If I understand the New Testament, though, its message is not that we are sinners in the hands of an angry God, but that we are sinners in the hands of a *loving* God. I know there are some terrifying pictures of God in the Bible, but the final, full revelation of God was Jesus. And Jesus made it crystal clear that God is like a father, a father who has unconditional love for His children. In fact, Jesus said that a human father's love for his offspring pales beside the unfathomable love of the eternal Father. Jesus, in life and teaching, was explicit: God is *for* us.

As I have intimated in some of my other letters, I think the biggest indictment against us as modern Christians is our joylessness. How can righteous, churchgoing people be so miserable, you ask? Easy! If our concept of God is askew, our hopes for joy are dashed! What we think about God is a key ingredient in our quest for joy. Our theology, you see, *is* important. If our God is an irate Tyrant, it's going to be tough to celebrate life. But if our God is a loving Father wishing the best for us, celebration will be a natural result.

One of my favorite verses is 1 John 4:18: "There is no fear in love, but perfect love casts out fear. For fear has to do with punishment, and he who fears is not perfected in love." I think John is telling us in this verse not to view God as the Celestial Policeman trying to whip us into shape, but as the Good Shepherd trying to draw us to Himself with love. We are to approach God not with fear, but with joy and gratitude.

I started thinking about all of this as I was reading the book *In Season and Out* this week. The book is written in journal form, and the author, John Leax, writes of his everyday activities as teacher, gardener, writer, husband, and father. One journal entry tells of an experience with his dog, Poon:

I saw Poon, foul-smelling, wagging his whole hind end in joy as I approached. A dumb beast, he understands grace. He knows, however much his bad habits annoy, I will not beat him for being a hound. He knows I will drag him to the back yard, turn on the hose, and wash him. Soaked and lathered, he will be humiliated; but cleansed, he will be allowed in the house.[17]

If old Poon can comprehend grace, why can't we humans? If he knows that John Leax will accept him even though he's a hound, why don't we know God will accept us even though we're human? When will we ever learn the glorious Good News that God knows us, accepts us, and wants us back in the house?

That realization has steadied me for a long time. I'm gradually coming out where the apostle Paul came out: "If

God is for us, who is against us?" (Romans 8:31). If the God of the universe is really on my side, what earthly problem or pain can ultimately defeat me?

Yours for making
the Good News good again,

Dad

SOLO FLIGHT

There is no shortage of advice these days. The modern media offer us a variety of experts ready to point us down the right path. Friends, preachers, psychiatrists, and family members are also eager to solve our problems and lead us to the good life. These letters themselves are but one illustration of the fact that you will be bombarded with "wise counsel" in the days ahead. We are all awash in a sea of suggestions.

Some of these suggestions are, of course, extremely helpful. Where would any of us be without the support and guidance of other people? Thankfully, the world gives us a

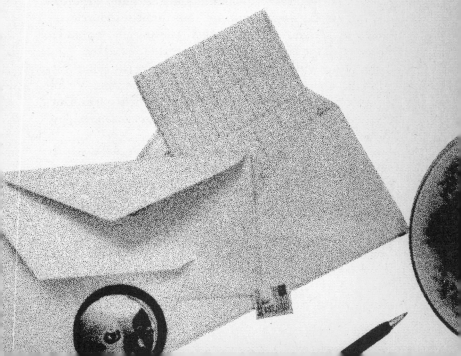

network of people who can give us invaluable tips on living life. That "no man is an island" is wonderful news!

But what I want to tell you in this letter is that life, ultimately, is a solo flight. Each of us has to fashion a personal blueprint for joy. All of life is a laboratory, and each of us is an experiment of one.

I have tried, in these epistles this year, to give you some of what I have found to be fundamental principles of joyful living. I think such things as trusting Christ, believing in a God of love, knowing and living Scripture, learning to be a servant, savoring the little things that life offers us, finding our special thing and doing it with enthusiasm, and some of the other subjects I've addressed are key planks in a life of joy.

But I also know that you need to find your own way in life. You each have your own treasure hunts to make. The best I can do is tell you where I've found treasure and let you go exploring on your own.

The good news about this scary, thrilling hunt for joy is that God is your Unseen Guide in the search. He wants to take you to abundant living. Ironically, we tend to listen to all the outside "experts" and fail to heed the promptings within us that are our truest treasure map. We read the advice columns. We check the horoscope. We follow the counsel of friends. We run to self-help gurus. But we never stop to ask, "Just what is it that makes me happy? Where is God wanting me to go?"

This subject is important to me because for years I followed the universal plan for happiness. I tried my best to do all the "right things": play football in high school, join clubs in college, work nine to five in a three-piece suit, look and believe and act like a successful person. To my disbelief, the "right things" were the "wrong things" for me. Following the commonly held plan for abundant living only left me miserable and isolated from the real me.

Just in recent years have I started trying to listen to God's whispers. Sometimes what I hear is rather surprising, but I'm learning to trust my inner promptings. I am learning that God most often speaks to me through my own desires, gifts, and circumstances.

Soren Kierkegaard once said, "The crowd is untruth." Only in the last few years have I verified that for myself. The crowd cannot tell me how to live, for the crowd doesn't know me nearly as well as I know myself. The message of the crowd is "Fit in. Conform. Be popular. Go along to get along." The *message* of the *heart* is "Be real. Stand apart. Be true to God and your unique self."

It's possible, I suppose, that learning to hear and heed God takes time, that only in midlife do humans have ears to hear His still, small voice. But it's also distinctly possible that I'm a slow learner! You might be able to take up wings and fly at a much earlier age than I did. On the chance that both of you are more perceptive than your father, I want to encourage you now to be different, to know that the crowded road is not always the best one to travel.

Shut off the television. Close the self-help book. Run from the glib advice-givers and follow the still, small voice within you. It will lead you to joy.

Flying high,

Dad

LAST WILL AND TESTAMENT

I, the undersigned, being somewhat sound of mind and body, do hereby bequeath to my offspring, Stacy Leigh Edwards and Randel Judson Edwards, the following wishes and promises.

Wishes

1. I wish for them lives of fascinating peculiarity. Let them follow their hearts to joy. Let them collect baseball cards, strum the guitar, watch birds, run marathons, crochet sweaters, or whatever else "winds their watch."

2. I wish for them a life partner as strong and loving as their mother. Let them, if they choose to marry, find a spouse who completes them and makes them whole.

3. I wish for them a faith in God that is alive and genuine. Let them find a spirituality that is real, that knows Christ intimately, that shuns the broad road of conformity. Let them be saturated in the love of God.

4. I wish for them a life's work that is a statement of who they are. Let them find a job that enables them to use their gifts and express their delight. May they be delivered from vocational treadmills, and find fulfillment.

5. I wish for them long days of reading good books, strolling through woods, fishing quiet streams, or any other peaceful activity that enables them to relax. Let them find ways to escape the pressures of the modern world.

6. I wish for them friends who know them and accept them for who they are. Let them find a few people who are kindred spirits, who understand their journey because they share the same road.

7. I wish for them children as fun and life-enriching as they have been. Let them, if they choose to have children, know the special love that only a parent knows. Let them have ample doses of the following: lumpy throats at awards ceremonies, nervous stomachs at ballgames and recitals, serious discussions about theology, feelings of wonder at the miracle of human development, watery eyes at the prospect of their offsprings' leaving.

To help those wishes become reality, I solemnly pledge to fulfill the following

Promises

1. I promise to let them live their own lives: to offer wisdom when sought and support when needed, but to allow them freedom to blaze their own trails.

2. I promise never to write another volume of letters dispensing fatherly counsel (unless, of course, the above-named children plead and beg for such correspondence).

3. I promise to continue to grow emotionally and spiritually, because the best gift I can give them is the gift of my best self.

4. I promise to be honest with them, to be open about my own struggles, hurts, and discoveries. I promise, in other words, to let them know I'm human.

5. I promise to love their mother with all of my being, to give them a living model of a marriage that works.

6. I promise to love God and to serve Him in the world, to try to give them an example of one whose life has been changed by grace.

7. Finally, I promise that I will always love them, that nothing in all of creation will sever the bond of affection I have for them. I promise that whatever their futures hold, I will always be a harbor to which they can safely sail.

Signed this 30th day of June, 1985, on the kitchen table.

Judson B. Edwards

NOTES

1. Robert Farrar Capon, *Bed and Board* (New York: Simon Schuster, 1965), p. 116.
2. Virginia Stem Owens, *The Total Image* (Grand Rapids: William B. Eerdmans, 1980), p. 81.
3. Robert Farrar Capon, *Hunting the Divine Fox* (New York: Seabury Press, 1974), p. 41.
4. Frederick Buechner, *The Alphabet of Grace* (New York: Seabury Press, 1970), p. 12.
5. H.B. Fox, *The 2000 Mile Turtle* (Austin: Madrona Press, 1975), p. 115.
6. Frederick Buechner, *Wishful Thinking* (San Francisco: Harper & Row, 1973), p. 20.
7. Ibid., p. 20.
8. Eric Hoffer, *Before the Sabbath* (New York: Harper & Row, 1979), p. 88.
9. W.P. Kinsella, *Shoeless Joe* (New York: Ballantine Books, 1982, p. 83.
10. Quoted in Carol Bly, *Letters from the Country* (New York: Penguin Books, 1981, p. 119.
11. Robert Young, *Religious Imagination* (Philadelphia: Westminster Press, 1979), p. 19.
12. Dr. George Sheehan, *Running & Being* (New York: Warner Books, 1978), p. 26.
13. Quoted in D. Bruce Lockerbie, *The Timeless Moment* (Westchester, IL: Cornerstone Books, 1980), p. 119.
14. Quoted in Lockerbie, p. 108.
15. Robert Farrar Capon, *The Youngest Day* (San Francisco: Harper & Row, 1983, p. 136.
16. Dr. George Sheehan, *This Running Life* (New York: Simon & Schuster, 1980), pp. 193-94.
17. John Leax, *In Season and Out* (Grand Rapids: Zondervan Publishing House, 1985), p. 123.